Readers' Reviews

***

"*A Mother's Homework from Heaven* is an excellent source of 'soul food' for mothers as they strive to nourish and nurture the gifts that God has blessed them with in their children. Our parish, Saint Augustine of Hippo, is considering giving it to parents as a part of our Faith Formation program."

Diane Sonneman, East Saint Louis, Illinois

***

"I think this book is a treasure for mothers, mothers-to-be and the next generation of mothers. It guides you along the spiritual path of motherhood, because it gives you concrete ways to raise your children in the faith."

Margaret Tolan, West Linn, Oregon

***

"What a beautiful, inspiring book! You certainly have written an interesting 'manual' for parents who will be eager and excited about reading the next page and the next page - and the next. It's a joy to read it. You have spent many prayerful hours searching scripture and immersing yourselves in His word and love."

Sister Ruthella Lamm, Saint Paul, Minnesota

A Mother's Homework from Heaven

***
*The Hand of God
is Closer Than You Think*

***
*Laurie Robbins & Mary Rogers
Cover by: Diane Robbins*

© 2024 Laurie Robbins and Mary Rogers

First published by AuthorHouse 8/13/04
Second Edition published by AuthorHouse 7/05/05

Scripture verses used in this book taken from:
1. The New Jerusalem Bible, copyright 1985 by Darton, Longman & Todd Ltd and Doubleday, a division of Bantam Doubleday Dell Publishing Group, Inc.
2. New Revised Standard Version - Catholic Edition, copyright Catholic Edition, © 2023 My Catholic Life! Inc. Powered by "Bible Gateway" A non-denominational Christian organization. The NRSV-CE is approved by the U.S. Bishops for Catholic use.

Contributors: Aaron, Kathleen, and Maggie Rogers

Cover Illustration: Diane Robbins:
Inspired by Brand X Pictures, Colin Anderson

All rights reserved.
No part of this publication may be reproduced, stored in a retrieval system, or transmitted in any form or by any means (including electronic, mechanical, photocopying, recording, or otherwise) without prior written permission of the authors.

*In dedication
to our husbands and children, who
have taught us so much and we love
beyond measure.*

***

*Steve, Sam, Amy, Rose,
Beth, Rebekah, Hannah,
Sarah, and Jonathan*

***

*Aaron, Patrick, Kathleen, Maggie,
and our little saints in heaven:
John Kirby, Baby Faith,
Baby Hope, and Baby Love*

Table of Contents

Opening 1
Blessed Trinity 3
    Leap into the Mystery 3
    We've Been Framed 10
God the Father 15
    Sacrificial Love 15
    Know Your Divine Dignity 24
    In the Face of Truth 31
The Father's Love 36
    The Ten Commandments 37
    Whims & Wants 38
    Regarding Names 44
    Holy Happenings 48
    Choosing to Honor 52
    Affirming Love 59
    An Attitude of Gratitude 64
    Sleep Sweet 70
    Let Us Respond 76
    Sharing Gifts 81
    People Come First 86
God the Son 90
    Pardon Me 90
    Mended Hearts 97
    Follow Me 101

- Be the Body of Christ 108
  - Corporal Works 110
  - Feed the Hungry 111
  - Satisfy the Thirsty 117
  - Welcome the Stranger 124
  - Clothe the Naked 129
  - Visit the Sick & Imprisoned 133
  - Lay to Rest 139
- The Spirit of Jesus 143
  - Living Jesus' Verbs 143
- Spiritual Works 144
  - Teaching with Kindness 145
  - Eyes on the Prize 151
  - Take Pause 157
  - Set Pride Aside 162
  - At the Center is Love & Grace 167
  - Pray for God's People 173
- God the Holy Spirit 179
  - I Want You 179
- Spotlight on the Spirit 188
  - Gifts of the Holy Spirit 189
  - We Accept It 190
  - Child-Smart/God-Smart 194
  - Matters of the Heart 201
  - Soar Like Eagles 206
  - Staying Power 210
  - Devotion 215

- Reverence & Awe ... 220
- Seven Gifts and a Friend ... 225

Fruits… Not Just Healthy but Holy ... 236
- The Spirit's Fruits ... 237
- A Modest Approach ... 238
- Strive to Improve ... 243
- Change of Heart ... 247
- Generous Love ... 251
- A Spirit of Joy ... 256
- Peace Prevails ... 262
- Waiting with Grace ... 269
- Cultivating Kind People ... 274
- Overcoming Self-Doubt ... 279
- Ever Faithful ... 284
- Avoid Insult to Injury ... 290
- Keeping Routines ... 295
- Holy Fruits ... 300

Women of the Beatitudes ... 306
- The Beatitudes ... 308
- Be Comforted ... 309
- Inherit the Earth ... 314
- Be Satisfied ... 318
- Receive Mercy ... 323
- See God ... 328
- Be the Children of God ... 332
- Kingdom of Heaven ... 337

Final Thoughts ... 342

Trust in Me	342
This is the Day	346
Closing	350
Epilogue	352
Raised to Praise	353
Love God by Serving Others	359
Our Bios	367
Endnotes	368

Opening

***

A Mother's Homework from Heaven, The Hand of God is Closer Than You Think was written for moms, by moms. This book began as an awkward attempt at a witty compilation of motherly memoirs meant to give moms a giggle. However, God transformed them, over the course of twenty-seven years, into a book whose "soul" purpose became helping moms, and their children reach a deeper relationship with each Person of the Blessed Trinity - God the Father, God the Son, and God the Holy Spirit. While writing this book, we took Jesus' words in Matthew 18:20 to heart, "For where two or three are gathered in My name, I am there among them." Therefore, while each memoir is personal, every reflection, activity, and final prayer that follows is a combined voice of two moms, with God in the center. This book aims to strengthen a mom's resolve to accept for herself, as well as to teach and model for her children, the immense love of the Blessed Trinity.

So, why did we name our book, *A Mother's Homework from Heaven?* It was inspired by the thought that God gives mothers homework, and that homework is to lend a helping hand by leading her children to Him. The realization that came with that is God is a mom's teacher. With that in mind, moms need to allow God to guide them as they would any teacher when taking a class, knowing that, as Saint Robert Bellarmine once said, "The school of Christ is the school of love. On the last day, when the general examination takes place… love will be the whole syllabus." Love is this book's syllabus too, and since God is love, its focus is to embrace the ways the Blessed Trinity calls us to love within our households of faith and beyond.

Isaiah 41:13 inspired the subtitle; *The Hand of God is Closer Than You Think.* It says, "For I, the Lord Your God, hold your right hand; it is I who say to you, 'Do not fear, I will help you.'" Moms, God is with you and your family, and His love is ever-present. When you give God one hand and your child the other, you are no doubt giving God a helping hand.

Moms, at the end of each chapter we have provided a page entitled, "Memos to Me" and "Pondering with Pictures." We recommend after each chapter giving yourself time to prayerfully reflect upon what you read. Then write down your thoughts or draw pictures about the ideas that moved you or could help you be the best mom you can be in your household of faith. So, mothers, before you begin reading the following pages, we invite you to fold your hands, bow your head, and pray for the wisdom to discern what can help you, and to take the rest as an affirmation of the good job you are already doing. When you are ready, so are we... and so is the Blessed Trinity.

Blessed Trinity

***

*"I believe though I do not comprehend,
and I hold by faith what I cannot
grasp with the mind."*
Saint Bernard

Leap into the Mystery

***

Mary's Memory

"Changing Lanes"

    It was a frigid November for Washington State, and we were making plans for Thanksgiving. My sister, Margaret, had invited Dad, Mom, and me down to Oregon for the holiday. It was snowing, and the roads were icy that year. The traffic reports said to stay home or sit in traffic for hours upon hours. Dad was a pilot and decided he would fly my mom and me to keep us off the roads. So, Dad borrowed his good friend's Learjet, and we were off in no time. I was excited because I got to sit in the cockpit with Dad. Mom sat in the back and read her book.

    The flight was incredible. I was a little disappointed because it was short, just an hour or so, and my dad was getting clearance to land in Portland. It was snowing heavily and was very cold, so the runway was slick. As the plane touched down, it started moving to the left side of the runway. Although Dad's demeanor was calm, I noticed that his hands were moving quickly over the plane's instruments. It didn't faze me; I was enjoying watching Dad do his thing.

Dad brought the plane to a stop on the far-left side of the runway. He had a look of relief on his face. Then, I heard Mom say from the back, "Gracious John, what are you trying to do, kill us?" I shot back, "Mom, he was just changing lanes!" Dad looked at me in disbelief, and then both my parents began laughing hysterically. I didn't understand what was so funny. Once my dad gathered himself, he turned to me and explained that the airplane was out of control as it slid across ice on the runway, and we nearly crashed. I was shocked, and a little embarrassed, but that day's events became my father's favorite story. He loved to tell of the day that his seventeen-year-old daughter trusted him so completely that it never dawned on her to be afraid. She had "Faith in her old dad!"

***

Heavenly Hint

"For we walk by faith, not by sight."
2 Corinthians 5:7

***

Reflection

God loves us and will patiently wait for us to have faith in Him. What does it mean to have faith in someone? Recall Mary in the above story. Her relationship with her dad had so much trust that Mary never thought her life was in danger. In Mary's eyes, her dad had everything under control. Truth be known, God has everything under control, and having faith means trusting God as much as Mary trusted her dad. However, trust is not always an easy task, for God is a mystery. Thankfully, trust comes easy for children. ¹Antoine de Saint-Exupéry, coincidentally also a pilot, and the author of *The Little Prince*, summed it up in a lovely manner when the Little Prince said, "It is only with the heart that one can see rightly; what is essential is invisible to the eye." How do we see what is essential to our hearts? We turn to God's word, for Jesus begins to explain in John 14:8,10-11:

> "Philip said to Him, 'Lord, show us the Father, and we will be satisfied.' 'Do you not believe that I am in the Father and the Father is in Me? The words that I say to you I do not speak on My own; but the Father who dwells in Me does His works. Believe Me that I am in the Father and the Father is in Me; but if you do not, then believe Me because of the works themselves.'"

This Scripture reveals that God the Father and Jesus His Son are one. They are two persons Divine, yet only one God. This is a definite mystery, as there is no human explanation for such a relationship.

Nine days after Jesus' ascension, scripture tells us in John 14:16-17 that He sent the Holy Spirit: "I will ask the Father, and He will give you another Advocate, to be with you forever. This is the Spirit of Truth, whom the world cannot receive, because it neither sees Him nor knows Him. You know Him, because He abides with you, and He will be in you." The Holy Spirit is the Spirit of Truth. He has guided and counseled the lives of those in both the Old and New Testaments, and He continues to guide and counsel us today.

Let us continue to reflect on what scripture tells us about the Blessed Trinity. Before Jesus left His disciples, He gave them a mission in Matthew 28:19, "Go, therefore, make disciples of all the nations; baptize them in the name of the Father and of the Son and of the Holy Spirit..." This scripture reveals to us that God is three Persons Divine and yet still the One True God. Accepting this takes faith, for faith requires leaping into the inexplicable mystery of God.

So, mothers, it is our job to help our children's hearts grow in faith and keep inviting them to build a relationship with God, even though they cannot physically see Him. Let us take the time to teach our children what it will take to have faith. Our children will have to trust enough to take a leap of faith and build a relationship with God the Father, God the Son, and God the Holy Spirit, to fully know the One True God.

At the center of the Blessed Trinity is love. The scripture verse in 1 John 4:8 says it best, "God is love." Saint Augustine explained it this way, He writes "...when I love something, there are three, I and what I love and the love itself." Love takes at least two people. The person doing the loving, the person receiving the love, and the act of love that is taking place between them. God is at the center of that love because He is love.

In our households of faith, moms are the subject, children are the object, and the acts of love flowing between them are our children's first example of God's love in action. As we love our children, we make visible to them an invisible God. In the school of love, mothers, we can take our children by the hand and guide them to the One True God with confidence. As the One True God is a mystery, it will be our job to keep inviting our children to leap into love, God's love.

***

Homework from Heaven

"The Shamrock"/ "Truths of the Trinity"

Materials: "The Shamrock"
- Scissors
- Glue
- One piece of green construction paper
- One piece of white computer paper
- Crayon, colored pencil, marker, or Sharpie™

What to Do: For Younger Children
1. Draw a shamrock that fills the green construction paper.
2. Either cut it out yourself or have your child cut it out depending on his or her age.
3. Do the same with the white paper but make it slightly smaller.
4. Glue the white shamrock onto the green shamrock. The green paper will act as a frame around the white one.
5. On the top leaf of the shamrock write: God the Father.
6. On the left leaf of the shamrock write: God the Son.
7. On the right leaf of the shamrock write: God the Holy Spirit.
8. Explain to your child that the Blessed Trinity is like this shamrock. It is all one shamrock, but it has three parts. Likewise, the Blessed Trinity is One God, but Who is three Persons.

***

Materials: "Truths of the Trinity"
- Bible or Youth Bible

What to Do: For Older Children
Here are some scripture verses to read with your children that reveal the truth of the Blessed Trinity. It is always a good thing to read scripture. We suggest reading the entire chapter to fully understand what God wants to reveal to you about Himself.

1. **Ephesians 1:15-17**
"I have heard of your faith in the Lord Jesus and your love toward all the saints, and for this reason I do not cease to give thanks for you as I remember you in my prayers. I pray that the God of our Lord Jesus Christ, the Father of glory, may give you a spirit of wisdom and revelation as you come to know Him…"

2. **John 15:26**
   "When the Advocate comes, whom I (Jesus) will send to you from the Father, the Spirit of Truth who comes from the Father, He will testify on My behalf."

3. **Acts 10:38**
   "That message spread throughout Judea, beginning in Galilee after the baptism that John announced: how God (Father) anointed Jesus of Nazareth with the Holy Spirit and with power; how He (Jesus) went about doing good and healing…"

4. **2 Corinthians 13:13**
   "The grace of the Lord Jesus Christ, the love of God, and the communion of the Holy Spirit be with all of you."

5. **Galatians 4:6**
   "Because you are children, God has sent the Spirit of His Son into our hearts, crying, 'Abba! Father!'"

***

Prayerful Pause

Dear Blessed Trinity,
Please give our children the desire to leap into the mystery of You and then hold on for all eternity.
Amen.

***
Memos to Me

_____
_____
_____
_____
_____
_____
_____
_____

***
Pondering through Pictures

We've Been Framed

***

Laurie's Story

"A Grandson's Puzzle"

My Dad and my son, Sam, loved doing jigsaw puzzles together when Sam was little. Dad would go to garage sales and buy all different types of puzzles. When we'd visit Dad, I would typically find Sam at a table with his grandpa, engrossed in putting together Dad's latest find. This tradition began when Sam was three.

Dad taught Sam to find all the edge pieces first, explaining that they are the frame that holds the puzzle together. Next, Dad taught Sam to fill in the middle pieces by teaching him to match the various shapes and colors. Over the years, it was a joy to watch Dad pour his love and attention over Sam as they sat and worked on what seemed like endless puzzles together.

***

Heavenly Hint

"He Himself is before all things, and in Him all things hold together."
Colossians 1:17

***

Reflection

We invite you to use your imagination to visualize a

photograph of your family arranged in a pyramid, with some on the bottom and one at the top. Now imagine that you have created a triangular-shaped puzzle out of that photograph. This triangular-shaped puzzle is the concept that we are building on. Now, metaphorically, picture that each member of your family is a middle piece of that puzzle. Something needs to hold the middle pieces together, and hopefully, it will be more than just a last name.

Remember how Sam learned that the edge pieces form a frame, which holds the puzzle together? Likewise, God desires to be a triangular frame that will hold the family together. How does God hold a family together? Each person of the Trinity takes a side, framing the family like the edge pieces frame a puzzle. Our family members are the middle pieces, and they must connect to God the Father, God the Son, and God the Holy Spirit to be complete or to live in God's absolute joy, for then, the fullness of God surrounds them.

For a family to experience God's complete joy, they must connect to each person of God. We know it takes all three Persons of God to make up the One True God. God the Father is not more essential than God the Son or God the Holy Spirit. In turn, God the Son is not more necessary than God the Holy Spirit or God the Father. Finally, God the Holy Spirit is not more crucial than God the Father or God the Son, for to experience the fullness of God, we need to have a relationship with each person of God.

To have a complete connection with the One True God will require intentionally having a relationship with each person of God. To have a complete connection with our family will require intentionally having a relationship with each family member. We must consciously engage with and love each person to fully connect as a family. God modeled families after Himself, for it takes all members to make up one complete family.

Within the family are individuals, but no one person is more valuable or more necessary than another, for as Saint Pope John Paul II told us, "To maintain a joyful family requires much from both the parents and the children... We are all equal in our ability to love." Celebrating each person's unique love within our family and within the Blessed Trinity is essential. That is how we stay framed and together. When loving our own families, who we do see, we love our God, who we cannot see.

***

Homework from Heaven

"Puzzle"

Materials:
- Construction paper
- Markers
- Ruler

What to Do:
1. Draw as big a triangle as you can, leaving about a one-inch border.
2. Allow each person of the Trinity to "take a side" by writing God the Father on one side of the triangle, God the Son on another side of the triangle, and God the Holy Spirit on the last side of the triangle.
3. In the middle of the triangle, draw in as many "puzzle" shapes as members of your family and then write each person's name in one of the shapes.
4. At the top of the page, write, "We are Framed in Love."
5. Discuss with your children how the love of God holds your family together.

***
Prayerful Pause

*Dear Father, Son, and Holy Spirit,
Thank You for framing our
Families in Your Love.
Amen.*

***
Memos to Me

_____
_____
_____
_____
_____
_____
_____
_____

***
Pondering through Pictures

God the Father

***

*"God loves each of us
as if there was only one of us."
Saint Augustine*

Sacrificial Love

***

Mary's Memory

"Asthma"

I was not an easy child. Chief among the reasons for this was my severe asthma. My parents taught me to accept myself and live without succumbing to self-pity. It took great personal sacrifice on their part. My parents gave me life twice, once when they said yes to God and He knit me in my mother's womb, and again as they affirmed me for who I was, despite my health.

My father was in the military, and, as a result, we moved frequently. It was also when smoking was fashionable, and problems like asthma and allergies were considered more psychological than physical. My father used to blow smoke rings to entertain my sister Margaret, but when he realized the "harmless little puffs" were causing her hives, he and my mother immediately quit smoking. It made him sick to think that the smoke hurt his baby girl. My parents went beyond quitting. No longer could friends or family smoke in our home. Thankfully, this happened before I was born. It would be one less thing my parents would have to cope with.

I was born in Colorado on Christmas Eve, 1963. I was a healthy and happy baby until I turned two. That was when my asthma kicked in - it was not uncommon for me to suddenly turn blue. What's more, I was allergic to most of the medications used back then, so it took some time before the doctors could treat my asthma effectively.

My mother sought help from the National Jewish Institute of Allergy and Immunology to improve my health. The Institute put me through an outpatient program, where my parents learned what it would take to deal with my severe asthma. They discovered that they would have to strictly control my environment if I was to be healthy. From that time on, they considered it their job to teach me how to manage my environment myself so that I could lead a "normal" life. My parents had the challenge of providing a "normal" life for my siblings while creating a lifestyle to control my asthma.

Life changed for the Chiltons. Either Mom or Dad had to be with me at all times. An unpredictable onset of asthma would frequently turn me blue; such an event required medicine and it had to be administered immediately. Then, it became a race to see if my medication would kick in before it became necessary to take me to the emergency room. My parents would often drive me to the hospital parking lot and wait to see if I started breathing better. Imagine what this did to their social lives, their sleep, and their emotional reserves!

By the time I was seven years old, my parents were already teaching me how to cope with my asthma. Here is a poignant example of why they felt the need to teach me these skills so early. I was just seven when my family traveled to Indiana to see my mom's family. I remember my parents allowing me to take a short walk with my cousin. We stepped off my grandparents' porch and walked past the next-door neighbor's house. By the time we reached the next house, I was struggling to breathe. I knew I needed help, so we turned around.

When we got back to my grandparents' house, I could hardly breathe and was already beginning to turn blue. There were many such occurrences along the way, and while it was not easy on the family as we adjusted, with their love and help I made enough improvement that just two short years later, I saw my father get misty-eyed for the first time. It was my ninth birthday, and I blew all the candles out on my cake. That was the first time I had enough air for this simple birthday tradition.

In the fifth grade, it was a big deal for my peers and me to participate in the twenty-one-mile bike-a-thon sponsored by our school. My best friend and I were very excited but thought for sure my parents would never allow me to do it. Surprisingly, they did!!

We spent a couple of months collecting sponsors and riding our bikes to build up our endurance. On the morning of the bike-a-thon, Mom had a terrible backache. My sister Margaret offered to ride along with me, but Mom wanted to go herself to guarantee my safety.

I remember a glorious day of fun with my best friend and my mom. I was proud that I successfully finished the race without having an asthma attack. You know, though, I never knew Mom's back hurt that day until Margaret told me years later. She unselfishly rode those twenty-one miles, so I could have that typical experience in my life. When I returned to school the following Monday, I enjoyed talking about the bike-a-thon along with all my classmates.

By seventh grade, I felt confident I had my asthma under control, so I told Mom and Dad that I was joining the basketball team. I could tell by their faces what was coming next, so I threw a huge fit to get my way. I'm not proud of it, but it worked.

That season, Mom went to every single practice and every single game. My asthma was troublesome, but we got through it. I still have the blanket that my mom crocheted as she watched me play. Stitch by stitch, my mother sat and endured long evenings, so I could have the experience of playing on a team. She affirmed her girl as I attempted to find myself while learning to live a typical life. I'm sure my mom and dad grew weary at times, but they were always there to challenge or encourage me along the way.

***

Heavenly Hint

"Let all that you do be done in love."
1 Corinthians 16:14

***

Reflection

God's love is sacrificial. When Jesus came from heaven at the moment of His conception, His sacrificial love began. God chose to limit Himself to a human body. As it says in John 3:16, "Yes, God loved the world so much that He gave His only Son so that everyone who believes in Him may not be lost but may have eternal life." God the Father so loved us that He chose to give us His Son, Jesus.

Our vocation begins at the moment of our child's conception, and so too does our sacrificial love, for God the Father calls us to sacrificial love and the responsibility that comes with a new life. He needs us to use the gifts He gave us precisely because He knew our children would need them.

Sacrificial love begins at home. It starts with all the little things we do as mothers. [2]Thérèse is known as "The Little Flower" because she imagined herself being a little wildflower in God's Garden, a flower that could easily go unnoticed. "Saint Thérèse embraced the ordinary and mundane aspects of daily life, finding holiness in the smallest acts of love and kindness." She found purpose in all the little things she did with love. She thought of her life as ordinary and, therefore, not worthy of attention. "Throughout her life, Saint Thérèse focused on prayer, self-sacrifice, and offering everything she did as an expression of love for God." But her small acts of love offered out of love for God caught His eye. What she called her little way did not go unnoticed, for she is a saint in heaven today.

In like fashion to Saint Thérèse's, a mother's life may appear to go unnoticed. Her life seems quite ordinary. A mother washes dirty faces, picks up and washes laundry, makes hundreds of dinners, taxis her children, and cleans bathrooms. There is nothing newsworthy there. Or is there? "Love and sacrifice are closely linked, like the sun and the light," says Saint Gianna. When a mom chooses small acts of sacrificial love, she links her vocation of motherhood to God, for love emanates from God, much like light emanates from the sun.

A mother teaches her children what God's sacrificial love is with every daily task. As in Mary's memory above, when her mom rode twenty-one miles on a bike in pain so that Mary could have a shared experience with her peers, or when she sat in the bleachers at every basketball practice, so Mary could be on the team despite her asthma.

Saint Francis de Sales is so practical when he says, "You learn to speak by speaking, to study by studying, to run by running, to work by working, and just so, you learn to love by loving." Teaching children to love comes as naturally as learning to speak, study, run, and work. As we mothers selflessly give of ourselves, we model God's love and teach our children how to love. For us to succeed, we will have to stay connected to God the Father, for as it says in 1 John 4:9-10, "This is the revelation of God's love for us, that God sent His only Son into the world that we might have life through Him. Love consists in this: it is not we who loved God, but God loved us…" just as we love our children.

***

Homework from Heaven

"Last Words Heard"/ "Heart's Delight"

What to Do: "Last Words Heard"

Mary came from a military family. Her dad was a pilot. Each time he left for a trip, Mary's mom taught Mary and her siblings to always tell their dad, "I love you" right before he left so that it would be the last words that he heard from them. As Mary got a little older, she asked her mom, "Why do you always tell us to say that?" Her mom was honest and answered, "Because there is no guarantee that he will return home." Once Mary's dad retired, they continued saying "I love you" when parting because they were old enough to recognize that you don't have to be in the military for something to happen. Given this reality, it extended beyond their dad to the entire family.

Mary's family believes that saying "I love you" should always be the last words spoken before parting ways. Through the years, Mary's family has continued to tell each other, "I love you" at every goodbye. Today this expression of love has become second nature even to Mary's mom's grandchildren. We recommend teaching this to your family and sharing this expression of love in your households of faith. You can never go wrong telling someone you love them.

***

Materials: "Heart's Delight"
- Construction paper or cardstock
- Marker
- Two jars or envelopes

What to Do:
1. Choose a specified period of time during which you will plan on doing something special for your children. You can choose to do things with them individually, or if a couple of your children both want to do the same thing, make that happen and count it. Keep it simple and keep the period of time you choose doable; it is not meant to overwhelm you. The goal is to have each child feel special during the specific time period that you have chosen.

    a. For example, Mary has three children and so decided that she would do something special for each of them within one month. Mary's ear perked up when she heard that Maggie and Kathleen played volleyball when they visited Beth. Then, Maggie mentioned that she wished she had a volleyball, and Kathleen agreed; Mary decided to buy them a volleyball and a net as their special thing.

    b. This example would have counted as Mary getting both of her girls something special. Now, Mary would only need to choose something special for Patrick before the month's end. Once she had taken care of Patrick, Mary would start over by selecting a new specified time that fits within her calendar. What's important is that your specified time works for you. Use whatever materials you have chosen to create a heart for each one of your children. Make sure to put their name on it.

2. Make as many hearts as you have children and write one child's name on each heart.
3. Place all the hearts into one container. The containers will keep track of who you've done something for and who you haven't. Label the containers, so you know which container is which. When you've completed that special something for a child, move their heart from one container to the other. Remember, this is meant to be a joy.

***
Prayerful Pause

*Dear Father,
Help us to focus our lives on reaching out to our children with Your sacrificial love.
Amen.*

***
Memos to Me

_____
_____
_____
_____
_____
_____
_____

***
Pondering through Pictures

Know Your Divine Dignity

***

Mary's Memory

"John Kirby"

I was at my twenty-week ultrasound when Aaron and I learned that our unborn son had hydrocephalus. Hydrocephalus is fluid on the brain, a condition that would compromise our son for the rest of his life. We were surprised when the midwife asked us to follow her into her office because that had never happened before. I sat in the chair beside her desk, and Aaron sat across from me. Our midwife suddenly stood between us, with her back to Aaron, and looked at me with intent. She then said, "Mary, you're looking at a difficult life ahead with this baby. It would be easier at this point to have an abortion. I think it's a good option. What do you think?" I was shocked! Aaron and I had already had a conversation and put in writing that that would never be an option for us. What was she thinking? Not only was she telling me it would be easy to end John Kirby's life, but she stood between Aaron and me as if Aaron wasn't even there.

When Aaron and I left her office, we were both furious! First of all, no one comes between Aaron and me because we are a team. Second, our baby would be given every chance to live. We decided to let her go. Not only because of the conversation we just had but because a midwife does not have the expertise for this kind of high-risk pregnancy. We needed a specialist to give our baby his best shot at life.

We spent the next eleven weeks closely monitoring our son's brain. In the thirtieth week, John Kirby's life hung in the balance. More water was on his brain, causing too much pressure, thus significantly increasing John's risk of brain damage. We had to decide whether or not to deliver John Kirby or give him one more week to grow inside the womb, thus increasing his chances of survival. We chose to give John Kirby one more week, thinking this would give him his best chance at life as it would give his lungs a little more time to develop.

During that week, it dawned on me for the first time that Baby John could have a headache. It made me cry to think that he could have been hurting before he ever entered the world, and I had the chance to hold and console him. It was then that I changed my prayer to God. Instead of asking for the miracle of his survival, at that moment, I asked God for His mercy. I could not stand the thought of my Baby John Kirby in pain.

He answered that prayer the very next day when I was at the computer with Laurie. It hit me that my baby had not moved all day. The doctor told us to come in immediately if our baby stopped moving because time would be of the essence to deliver him safely. Aaron took me straight to Urgent Care. The ultrasound technician could not find our baby's heartbeat. Rather than telling us, the doctor chose to send us straight to the maternity ward of our local hospital in the event that it could be a mistake. There, a second ultrasound took place and with sorrow, the doctor told us that our sweet baby boy had died within me.

After a long delivery lasting four days, John Kirby was born. When the doctor asked Aaron if he wanted to cut the cord, I expected his typical answer, "No." He surprised me, however, and cut John Kirby's cord. When I asked him later why he chose to cut Baby John's cord, his answer was beautiful, "Cutting the cord is symbolic of a father's role. The father separates the child from dependency on the mother to prepare him for independence in the world. I didn't need to act out that symbolism with the other children because I had them for the rest of their lives. But I don't get Baby John; the symbolism is all I had. So, I cut the cord, and I gave him to God."

When I handed Baby John to Aaron, Aaron cradled him tenderly in his arms and carried him to the window. Aaron always shows his newborns the world. I loved that he carried out this ritual for his newest son. Later on, when Aaron's parents arrived at the hospital, I noticed how carefully Aaron placed Baby John into their arms so as not to harm a hair on his head. In our short seven hours with our son, it was evident how very much Aaron loved both his son and his God.

After both of Aaron's parents held John Kirby, his mom handed him back to me. I cuddled him close and sang the lullaby that my mom sang to me because I sang it to all my babies. Eventually, the nurse told Aaron and me that volunteers make clothes and blankets for stillborn babies, so the parents can have something to take home with them. She asked if we would like that for John Kirby. Aaron and I agreed, and I handed Baby John to her. About half an hour later, she returned, rolling John Kirby in the hospital bassinet, dressed in a cute little outfit with a small blanket under him. She was carrying a beautiful satin box. In it were pieces of his hair, his hospital bracelet, ink prints of his hands and feet, and a prayer card with his height and weight on it. We could not hold Baby John again because he was so fragile. We took pictures of him, just as we did with our other babies.

When it came time to leave, the nurse rolled John Kirby out, to remove the outfit so we could take it home. She came back with him in the bassinet, his tiny body covered with a blanket. She also had photos of him for us. We knew our time with our baby was winding down. Aaron and his parents packed our belongings as I got dressed. Before leaving, I leaned over my John Kirby and asked God to take care of him until we could be together again. I was crying. I bent down to kiss his sweet head and one of my tears fell under his eye and began rolling down his cheek. It felt as if we were both crying at our final goodbye.

Though difficult, Aaron and I spent the following days planning a funeral so our family and friends could say goodbye to our son, to whom they never had the opportunity to say hello. Together, we celebrated God's everlasting love for our beloved John Kirby and his return home to the Father. [3]Here is the responsorial hymn sung at John Kirby's funeral, based on Jeremiah 31:3, "I have loved you with an everlasting love, I have called you, and you are Mine."

On John Kirby's 21st birthday, the girls invited Aaron and I to dinner. Maggie asked us to tell her about her brother's birth because she was too young to remember it. So, Maggie got on her computer and pulled up this book. Maggie read the story aloud to Aaron, Kathleen, and me. We all cried. When she finished reading, I asked, "How do you miss a life that you never got to live with someone? And yet, I do."

***

Heavenly Hint

"You created my inmost self, knit me together in my mother's womb. For so many marvels I thank you; a wonder am I, and all Your works are wonders."
Psalm 139:13-14

***

Reflection

To our Almighty Father, every life is precious. In fact, in God's eyes, every person has immeasurable worth. Pope Benedict XVI reminded us of this when he said, "Each of us is the result of a thought of God. Each of us is willed. Each of us is loved. Each of us is necessary." Mary and Aaron's reaction to John Kirby's precarious health and their refusal of an abortion illustrates this well. Not only did Mary and Aaron choose to continue the pregnancy, but even in death, they honored the dignity of John Kirby's life. Aaron used the symbolism of cutting the cord to acknowledge that the soul of his son John Kirby returned to God. In Aaron's heart, he did his best to baptize his son, but not knowing this, Mary asked the priest when he arrived, "How do we baptize our baby?" The priest explained that the Baptism of Intent achieved this. Mary and Aaron had every intention of baptizing John Kirby; God honored that intent. At that moment, Mary knew that their son and their other three miscarried infants, Baby Faith, Baby Hope, and Baby Love were baptized. Mary found peace in that knowledge. We hope all parents who have lost their infants will feel the same comfort that Mary and Aaron did when they heard this.

Aaron and Mary then turned their attention to celebrating the dignity of John Kirby's life with family and friends at his funeral and luncheon. During the luncheon, several ladies came to Mary with tears in their eyes and told her that getting to be at John Kirby's funeral meant so much to them. It gave them the chance to say goodbye in a ceremonial way to the babies they had lost. Mary found solace in this. She had been struggling with why she lost Baby John, but when the ladies shared that her baby's funeral had relieved the grief they were holding onto, Mary found purpose in John Kirby's short little life in a new way. For as Pope Benedict XVI said, "...each life is willed and is necessary." John Kirby's life was necessary not only for Mary and her family but also to bring healing to others.

Moms, dignity is a gift from our Lord. When Mary's family got together on John Kirby's twenty-first birthday, they were honoring his life. God's love is sacrificial. At the moment of Jesus' conception, His sacrificial love began. God chose to limit Himself to a human body. As it says in John 3:16, "Yes, God loved the world so much that He gave His only Son so that everyone who believes in Him may not be lost but may have eternal life." God the Father so loved us that He chose to give us His Son, Jesus.

***

Homework from Heaven

"Baby of Mine"

Materials:
- Your child's baby books
- Photographs of your child growing up
- Childhood treasures and clothes

What to Do:
1. At every birthday, sit down with your child and look through his/her baby books, photographs, and baby treasures and clothes. Tell them stories about how much happiness and love they bring to the family.
2. As part of the celebration, ask your child what new thing they are interested in. Celebrate each child's uniqueness by discovering what they love and if possible, help them to pursue it. Join them, if they would like you to participate. For example, Laurie took cake decorating classes with her daughter, Rose, because Rose had a great love for baking.

***

Prayerful Pause

*Dear Father,
Help our children to know their dignity,
and the dignity of others as well.
Amen.*

***
Memos to Me

_____

_____

_____

_____

_____

_____

_____

***
Pondering through Pictures

In the Face of Truth

***

Mary's Memory

"A Sweet Character"

When I was teaching second grade, I encountered a little boy who was a real character. With only kindergarten and first grade under his belt, he had already been labeled a "lost cause." He was doing his best to fulfill this prophecy too. Granted, he was a handful, but his underlying character was very sweet.

Each time I had to discipline him for his behavior, I started with his name and reminded him that I loved him but that we needed to talk about what he had just done. I'd ask him why he chose to do what he did and then listen to his answer. Then, we'd talk about a better way to handle the situation. Often, I would end by saying, "You are such a good person. I know you can do better next time." This boy, who believed he was a troublemaker, was now confronted with God's truth that he was not only good but worthy of being loved. By June, after nine months of hearing the truth about himself, this same boy who in September had walked in with an angry heart, skipped out of class with a joyful one. He had turned around so completely that this sweet boy acknowledged in writing that he loved me before he left for third grade. That sweet boy never actually saw God walk into my classroom, but through our love for one another, he experienced Him.

***
Heavenly Hint

*"So then, let us be always
seeking the ways which lead to peace.
and the ways in which we can
support one another."*
Romans 14:19

***
Reflection

God does what is right at all times. He does not change His order of things depending upon His mood or the situation at hand. We must do the same for our children by teaching them the difference between right and wrong. In 1 Corinthians 13:6, it states, "It (Love) does not rejoice in wrongdoing, but rejoices in the truth." Because we love our children, we must be vigilant in our pursuit of the truth, which is that God the Father created our children, and they are good. This goodness is what the second-grade boy learned in Mary's classroom. Hearing the truth about himself turned him around.

Mary did what was right by expecting the boy's inappropriate behavior to change, yet vigilantly helping him face God's truth about his inner goodness. By helping her student accept his inner goodness Mary helped her student find his joy again. As Saint Pope John Paul II said, "God made us for joy. God is joy, and the joy of living reflects the original joy that God felt in creating us." It is that joy that allowed a once angry boy to leave Mary's classroom skipping out with a joyful heart.

It is a mother's job to foster her child's goodness through loving acceptance of the person that God the Father created. However, the Father's gift of free will, coupled with the fact that our children will test us to determine what is right from what is wrong, will require a balance between affirming their goodness and correcting their choices. This balance is just what Mary provided for the student in her classroom.

A mother's response to her children's testing could determine whether or not her children will become happy and obedient children of God. It will also test our patience because we must be consistent like Mary was in the story. If we are not consistent, then the testing will get worse. If a child finds that something works once but does not the second time, they will escalate their means of getting their way. At that point, affirming their goodness could potentially backfire. Consistency is the key. Just as God does not change the order of things on us, we should not change the order of things on our children. By following God's example and staying within the order we establish, coupled with affirming their goodness when correcting their choices, we will reap the benefits of our labor. We are not saying this will be easy, but we will be glad we did it in the end, and so will our children.

***

Homework from Heaven

"Discipline with Love"

What to Do:

The next time you need to discipline your child, remind yourself to affirm him or her simultaneously. Consider using Mary's approach with the boy in her classroom. Remind your child of your constant love and correct the choice they have made. Include a consequence when needed. Then tell your child what a good person they are and that you know they can do better. You will be amazed at the results!

***
Prayerful Pause

*Dear Father,
Please help us imitate Your consistency, as we teach our children the difference between right and wrong while always affirming their goodness in the process.
Amen.*

***
Memos to Me

_____
_____
_____
_____
_____
_____
_____
_____

***
Pondering through Pictures

The Father's Love

***

*"It is not hard to obey when
we love the One whom we obey."*
Saint Ignatius

A Mother's Eyes

***

God is our Father, and we are His beloved children. God sent us the Ten Commandments straight from heaven to teach us how to love Him and each other. For as it says in 1 John 4:19, "We love because He first loved us." Obeying the Commandments is not meant to be a challenge. They are meant to enrich our lives and show us how to love each other better.

In this section of the book, we will put a unique twist on God's Ten Commandments. Our twist will be to look at the Ten Commandments with fresh eyes. To see them through the eyes of a mother in particular.

It is important to take God's commandments literally, but we should not stop there. For example, Mothers are the heart of the home and when a mother looks at God's commandments with fresh eyes, a mother's eyes, we hope it will enrich the relationships within her household of faith. So, mothers, let's have a look.

The Ten Commandments

***

"I am the Lord your God... you shall have no other gods before Me."

"You shall not make wrongful use of the name of the Lord your God…"

"Remember the Sabbath day, and keep it holy."

"Honor your father and your mother…"

"You shall not murder."

"You shall not commit adultery."

"You shall not steal."

"You shall not bear false witness against your neighbor."

"You shall not covet your neighbor's wife…"

"You shall not covet your neighbor's house… or anything that belongs to your neighbor."

Exodus 20:2-3,7-8,12-17

Whims & Wants

***

Mary's Memory
"Mountain of Food"

I was a senior in high school and student president of Campus Ministry. Thanksgiving was coming up, and our club decided to have a food drive. Our goal was to fill the upper section of the chapel. It was a lofty goal but attainable. As the food drive drew to a close, the club members and I decided to meet after volleyball practice on the Friday before Thanksgiving break. We planned to load the food that the school collected into the back of my dad's truck. Then, several of us would drive it down to the food bank. We knew it would take some time because we had already met our goal and then some. It was amazing how gracious the families from the school had been.

That Friday, when volleyball practice ended, I headed over to my dad's truck because that's where the club members and I had agreed to meet. The plan was to pile in, and I'd drive us all to the chapel. When I got there, only a few people showed up. The rest had gone home. I was concerned because I knew that this meant it was going to take some serious time!

As the four of us drove over to the chapel, we started talking about that night's football game. It was a home game, and as it turned out, an important game for us to win. To my dismay, the club members decided that they would load until kick-off and then return when the game was over. I told them that that would make it too late for the delivery to the food bank. They understood and committed to returning to help at half-time. So, we started loading up the truck, but we hadn't even packed a quarter of the food at the time of kick-off. Everyone left but assured me they would return.

There I stood, alone. I felt deflated and was nearly in tears, but when I looked at the food and remembered that the food bank was waiting for the delivery, it was then that I knew that I had no alternative but to start loading, so I did. I loaded and loaded and loaded. Half-time came and went, and I was still alone. I was getting worried. It was starting to get late, and the food bank was going to close soon. It was then that one of my teachers, who had been supervising the football game, noticed that someone was taking things out of the school building and loading them into a truck. Bewildered, he came over to see what was going on. I explained the situation. He got mad and left in a huff. It surprised me that he just left, but I kept loading the food. Before I knew it, he came back with four or five other teachers to help me. While we continued to load, he went to his office and called the food bank, asking them to stay open for us. Thankfully, they agreed.

Once we got all the food loaded, my teacher offered to go with me to the food bank but suggested that I call my folks first to explain the situation. My parents agreed to let me make the delivery despite how late it was and were thankful for my teacher's help. So, we got in the truck and left for the food bank. When we had finished unloading all the food and were on our way back, I told my teacher how relieved I was. He smiled at me and told me how proud he was that I didn't give up against that mountain of food, as now much of the greater community would have a Thanksgiving. I told him how grateful I was for his help and for finding the other teachers to help me. When I talked to my teacher after Thanksgiving break, I told him how sore I had been after loading and unloading all that food. He laughed and said he was sore too, but we both agreed that the whole ordeal was worth it.

***
Heavenly Hint

"Instruct a child in the way he should go, and when he grows old he will not leave it."
Proverbs 22:6

***
Reflection

God's first commandment is, "I am the Lord your God... you shall have no other gods before Me." It is one of the most natural things to want to give our children the best of everything that this world has to offer. It is also natural for our children to want this. It is not that our children are bad people. We have already established their goodness. It is just that they are growing up through the developmental stages of life. They start by thinking of themselves as the center of the universe. Tempering their me-centered world and broadening it to the bigger world around them bit by bit is how we promote them putting God first in their lives. It says in Psalm 37:4, "Make Yahweh your joy and He will give you your heart's desires." God knows what is in our children's hearts and He also knows what our children need. When God is our children's joy, they will not desire what they see in the world because their hearts will be focused on God.

Mothers, we need to fight our instinct to show our children how much we love them by providing for all of their whims and wants. Providing for their every heart's desire may make them happy in the now, but it may not in their future. It is hard to put God first if our children are consumed with what the world touts they need. In truth, our children need God. Teaching and modeling self-denial instead, will be more beneficial to our children. Self-denial means putting the need for the bigger picture ahead of our current whims and wants. Saint Benedict expressed this well when he said, "No one should follow what he considers to be good for himself, but rather what seems good for another." That is what we mean by self-denial, teaching our children to put aside their own whims and wants and consider what is best for everyone in the situation.

Mary's Memory above showed what it means to exercise self-denial. The untold piece of the story is that Mary lived a half-hour from her high school, and her parents typically worked on Friday nights. This concerned Mary's parents because they would not be available to Mary should she need help. Therefore, they did not allow her to go to the football games. This particular Friday, Mary's parents permitted it because she would already be at the high school working with the food donations. However, once left alone with the mountain of food, Mary chose not to attend the game. She denied herself going to the game with her friends. In doing this, Mary was honoring the first commandment by putting the things of God first, which was to provide Thanksgiving to families in need.

Remember that Mary was a senior in high school in her story. Mary's parents had taught her by that time that she was no longer the center of the universe. They had walked her through the stages of life and helped her to see that God comes first. Moms, let us do the same with our children. Let us teach our children that they are not the center of the universe - God is.

***

Homework from Heaven

"Family Vacations"

What to Do:

It is a great joy to do the things that make our children and family happy. One such example is family vacations. Typically, when we think of family vacations, we think of going somewhere where the family plays and relaxes together. We suggest you consider teaching your children the importance of charitable acts by taking a family vacation or two like the one a family took when Mary taught in a Catholic high school. Her student's family took their summer vacation to Calcutta, India, and worked with Saint Teresa of Calcutta who worked with the poorest of the poor. She founded the Order of the Missionaries of Charity. Her order brought people off the streets who were dying and gave them a place to die with dignity by taking care of their needs and loving them tenderly. Saint Teresa of Calcutta believed, "A life not lived for others is not a life."

When the family returned, they put a video together to share their vacation and answer questions about their experience. Every family member agreed that it was one of the most challenging things they have ever done physically and emotionally. They also declared it was one of the best experiences of their lives. This approach to self-denial can teach children that not everyone has what they do. It is one way to help them see that they are not the center of the world. Tailor this kind of family vacation to the age of your children. True, not every family can fly to India; however, our communities, or communities near us, can always use our help.

***

Prayerful Pause

Dearest Father,
May we always praise, thank,
and adore You alone, through self-denial
and charitable acts, as You are the
One True God forever and ever.
Amen.

***
Memos to Me

_____

_____

_____

_____

_____

_____

_____

***
Pondering through Pictures

Regarding Names

***

Mary's Memory

"Caffeine"

Kathleen is a problematic name for little ones to say. They can't wrap their tongues around going from the sound of "th" directly to the sound "l." Consequently, Kathleen comes out caffeine. When Kathleen was young, and her peers would hear a little one calling her Caffeine, they'd tease Kathleen by saying that Caffeine fits her and then laugh. It grew old over time, as Kathleen loves her name. Even at that age, Kathleen wished that people would respect her name because it was unique, like her, which made her feel special. She thought it was one thing when a sweet little one mispronounced her name, and yet another when friends used the mispronunciation to make fun of her. This experience taught Kathleen the importance of a person's name. To this day, Kathleen takes a genuine interest in people's names and makes sure to pronounce them correctly and treat the name and the person with respect.

***

Heavenly Hint

"A good name is to be chosen rather than great riches, and favor (respect) is better than silver or gold."
Proverbs 22:1

***
Reflection

God's second commandment is, "You shall not make wrongful use of the name of the Lord your God..." God's name should only be said in prayer or respectful conversation. We should teach our children to revere the name of God for scripture tells us in Psalm 34:3, "O magnify the Lord with me, and let us exalt His name together." There truly are no words to respect God's name enough. Blessed Henry Suso told us, "We should bow in reverence to God's name." We completely agree with Blessed Henry Suso because God's majesty is beyond our comprehension.

In His majesty, that God would even think to create each of us shows His boundless love. It is in that same love that our children should be taught to respect each other's names for we are all His beloved children. A person's name is their identity. When a child disgraces another child's name, they disgrace the person. For example, with Kathleen, children innocently changed her name, and she thought it was endearing until others jumped on the name Caffeine and used it to make fun of her.

The Rogers family has established a tradition for the firstborn boys in the family. Mary's father-in-law's name is Mark Kirby, and he goes by Kirby. Her husband's name is Mark Aaron, and he goes by Aaron. Finally, Mary's son's name is Mark Patrick James, and he goes by Patrick. They are all proud to have this connection with one another. Often, families choose to name their children after relatives because those people are precious to them. If we honor the names of relatives, is it not equally important to honor the name of God? Just as we want people to honor our names, we must teach our children to honor God's name. Mary taught her children that the worst of all the bad words is to say God's name without prayer or love. Let us all do the same.

***

Homework from Heaven

"A Child's Name"

Materials:
- Computer paper
- Construction paper
- Markers, crayons, colored pencils, paint, stickers
- Glue

What to Do:
1. On the computer paper, write an acrostic using your child's name. For example:

   H onest
   A rtistic
   N ice
   N eeded
   A thletic
   H opeful

2. Glue the acrostic to the center of the construction paper.
3. Decorate around your child's name.

***

Prayerful Pause

*Dear Father,
Please help us give Your name
and everyone's name the love
and respect they are due.
Amen.*

***
Memos to Me

_____
_____
_____
_____
_____
_____
_____
_____

***
Pondering through Pictures

Holy Happenings

***

Laurie's Story

"Sacred Sundays"

Growing up, Sundays were sacred at our house. If we ever tried to argue about going to church, Mom would routinely say, "Come on, you know what Dad expects. There is only one reason good enough to miss Mass, and that's if you're on your deathbed!" She said it lightheartedly, but we knew Mom and Dad meant it. I never remember a Sunday when our family did not go to church. We would always get there early because if we didn't, my family would not get to sit together as the nine of us took up an entire pew.

Dad also honored the Sabbath by not doing work of any kind, which allowed us time to make fond family memories. That family time created many "holy happenings." Like when we lived in Nebraska, sometimes we'd go to our grandparents' cabin on the lake and spend the day, take a trip to the zoo, or just take a family drive. I can still feel the cold when my dad would take us older kids out sledding while Mom would stay behind with the younger kids. When we got home, Mom always had a roaring fire in the fireplace and homemade soup to help thaw us out. I look back with such joy on those days we spent together.

***
Heavenly Hint

"For in six days the Lord made heaven and earth, the sea, and all that is in them, but rested the seventh day; therefore the Lord blessed the Sabbath day and consecrated it."
Exodus 20:11

***
Reflection

    In the third commandment, God tells us to "Remember the Sabbath day, and keep it holy." Going to church as a family on Sunday is part of God's day. It is how He invites us to share in His holiness and how we show God that we love and glorify Him above all else. Saint Jean Marie Vianney clearly tells us that "Sunday is the property of our good God; it is His day, the Lord's day. He made all the days of the week: He might have kept them all; He has given you six and has reserved only the seventh for Himself." Going to church allows us to worship with our faith community, but we do not have to stop there when making Sunday sacred.

    Another way to make Sunday sacred is to invite people we love to our homes. In particular, we can take the time to attend to our parents or grandparents. Just as God weekly gathers His people together to spend time with Him around His Holy Table, we, in turn, can gather our family and friends around our table. Mary and Aaron have a standing invitation for Papa to come for Sunday supper. Through the years, it has evolved into watching a movie after dinner. We call it Dinner and a Movie. Every Sunday, Aaron's dad comes at 3:00 P.M., and shortly after, the family eats supper. An early supper allows time for visiting but also gives time for us to pick a movie for all to enjoy. It is a fun tradition that brings the family together on a day set aside for "holy happenings."

***

Homework from Heaven

"Holy Habit"

What to Do:
1. Take your family to church every Sunday. Make it an unshakable habit.
2. If there is a Sunday brunch or donuts afterward, plan on taking the time to stay and enjoy it. This opportunity helps the whole family to build friendships with their church community.
3. Consider giving a standing invitation to your parents or grandparents for Sunday supper or bringing dinner and a movie to your parents or grandparents if it is difficult for them to get out.

***

Prayerful Pause

Dear Father,
Your Sabbath is so important to us
that we will observe each Sunday with a
joyful heart.
Amen.

***
Memos to Me

_____
_____
_____
_____
_____
_____
_____
_____

***
Pondering through Pictures

Choosing to Honor

***

Laurie's Story
"It Was My Turn"

My dad was healthy his whole life. My mom even said that he never had a reason to go to the doctor, with the one exception of the time he got a fleck of metal in his eye. Then, one day Mom saw Dad walking a little wobbly. Mom asked, "What's the matter?" Dad said that he thought he had gotten up too quickly from his chair. Dad walked down the short hall and went into one of the bedrooms. Mom hesitated, and then decided to follow him. When she entered the room, she found him slumped over the bed. Mom asked, "What's wrong?"

"Nothing."

"What are you doing?"

"I'm just resting."

Mom knew better and immediately called her brother Larry who lived close by. When he answered, Mom said, "Get your butt over here. I need your help - I think I need to call 911 for Robert."

Larry sped right over, saw my dad, and agreed. Mom called 911. When the four firemen arrived, Dad had somehow gotten himself to the bathroom. The firemen were coming up the stairs when Dad came out of the bathroom. One of the firefighters turned to my mom and said, "We can't take him to the hospital."

"Why not?"

"Because he can walk."

"He can barely walk."

"We're not going to take him."

The firemen headed back down the stairs and as one of them passed Mom, he whispered, "I think he had a mini stroke."

"You're still not going to take him?!"

"Nope, he can walk." Then the firefighters left. My mom and Larry were shocked and realizing that they were on their own made a dash for the emergency room.

After sitting in the waiting room for what felt like forever, they called Dad back. The doctor evaluated him and decided to run several tests including an MRI. When the test results came back, the doctor informed my parents that Dad had spinal meningitis. He further explained that the MRI showed that Dad had ten abscesses in his brain. They immediately put Dad on medication and kept him at the hospital for about a week. When it came time to discharge Dad, the doctor told Mom that he needed further care in a facility. The doctor asked Mom where they should send Dad. Mom answered, "Mother Joseph Care Center." When Dad heard the plan, he refused. He wanted to go home. The doctor asked Mom, "Do you have a full bathroom on the main floor?"

"No, it's upstairs."

"Then he can't go home. We can't risk him walking up and down stairs."

"What am I supposed to do?"

"Do you have another family member who has a full bathroom on the same floor where Robert would be staying?"

"Yes, my daughter."

So, mom called and explained the situation, and asked if they could come to our house until Dad was well enough to go home. I talked to Steve and he wholeheartedly agreed that my mom and dad should come and live with us.

So, I quickly turned our den into a bedroom. All the kids cheered when they heard Grandma and Grandpa were going to live with us for a while. Dad's healing was slow, but on the upside, it was wonderful getting to spend time with my parents. Mom and I loved being a team as we took care of Dad together.

When Mom and Dad's anniversary rolled around, Dad said he wanted to spend it at home. Mom agreed with the intention of coming back later that day. Little did she know that Dad was planning on staying. So, stay they did. Dad was on multiple medications and some of them were complicated in their delivery.

As Mom was not in the medical field, she wasn't confident with having that responsibility alone. She didn't want to further compromise Dad with a mistake. So, she asked me to come up and help her, saying, "He's not going to die on my watch!" I agreed and stayed for a few days until she got the hang of it. By the grace of God, along with the medication, Dad fully recovered.

Years later, when Mom and I were remembering this time, she got teary. Mom told me that I honored them big-time by letting Dad heal at our house. It gave her peace of mind, knowing she wasn't in it alone - she had help. I said, "Of course! You two always sacrificed for us our whole lives, it was my turn. I was happy to do it."

***

Heavenly Hint

"With all your heart honor your father, never forget the birth pangs of your mother. Remember that you owe your birth to them; how can you repay them for what they have done for you?"
Sirach 7:27-28

***

Reflection

God's fourth commandment is "Honor your father and your mother..." Honoring our parents is an important lesson in life. Mothers and fathers make daily sacrifices for their children. Children may not understand the sacrifices or the reasons for the decisions made, but they do not have to. We do not always understand God's ways either, and yet, we honor and respect Him, nonetheless.

When we are loved like God loves, we honor people not only because He asks us to but because we want to. We recognize the sacrifices behind their love and choose to honor them for it. Laurie does this in her story above. Laurie's mom and dad needed help. Her dad was sick but wanted the dignity of healing at home. Given his situation, the next best solution was staying with Laurie. She did not hesitate. Her parents had shown her what it meant to love her entire life. They made countless sacrifices to give Laurie and her six siblings an amazing childhood. Laurie's parents modeled the Father's love and she knew that it was her turn to give back at least an ounce of all the love they had given to her.

We recognize that not everyone has parents as amazing as Laurie's. However, we also acknowledge that God's love for us can help us overcome difficult childhoods. Pope Francis acknowledges this when he says, "There are many saints who demonstrate that even if one comes from a difficult childhood without good parents, hope can still be found in Christ and the mission received from Him... Many saints - and many Christians - after a painful childhood lived a bright life, because, thanks to Jesus Christ, they were reconciled with life." If we are going to reconcile with life, we will first have to reconcile with ourselves.

When someone was raised in a home of hurtfulness their hearts protect themselves. For us to open those hearts up again we must forgive the people who caused us to close them in the first place, especially if the hurt comes from a parent because the hurt runs deep. It is difficult to let go of such hurt because it can fester inside of us and leave us angry. We can easily relive it over and over again or bring it up to our parents repeatedly, thus causing anguish for everyone. However, Proverbs 10:12, tells us that, "Hatred stirs up strife, but love covers all offenses." In order to end this vicious cycle, it takes finding a way to forgive our parents and move past the hurt. In this, love can fill us, and our lives will become sweeter.

This becomes our challenge. Forgiving our parents will not come easy but praying for them will help. Keep in mind that they might not have been the parents they wanted to be. Our forgiveness might help them to forgive themselves and possibly lead them to ask us for forgiveness. Even if they do not, our forgiving them will move us closer to reconciling the hurt in our own hearts. Either way, reconciliation is what will make life sweeter. So, as we pray for a forgiving heart toward our parents, may we remember to also pray that God will help us to be the best version of ourselves for our own children.

When we ask God for help, He gives us what we need to be great moms. It will not come without challenges, for motherhood always comes with challenges, but it should also come with love and respect. When we love and respect our children, and model it after the love and respect God gives us, they not only know it - but also feel it in their souls. So, moms, let us love our children hard and may this love be the catalyst upon which they, like Laurie, choose to honor us.

***

Homework from Homework

"How Can I Help You?"

What to Do:

1. Teach your younger children the importance of asking people, "How can I help you?" thus showing love and respect to others, especially family members like Mom and Dad. Honor their question by telling them ways they can be helpful. Regularly remind your children to ask this question so that it becomes a habit.
2. Teach your older children to love and respect their grandparents by paying attention to how they could use help around their homes and then just help them without having to be asked.
3. Teach your younger children to love and respect others enough to choose to leave a place looking better than when they arrived. For example, when visiting someone else's house, teach them to not only pick up after themselves but also the area around them. If they are there for supper,

teach them to clear their own plate after supper, then offer to help with the dishes. Hopefully, it won't be necessary to remind your older children as it will have already become a habit.

***

Prayerful Pause

Dear Father,
Honoring our mothers and fathers
is a privilege. Please help us remember to
ask, "How can I help?" always filled with
love and respect in our hearts.
Amen.

***
Memos to Me

_____

_____

_____

_____

_____

_____

_____

***
Pondering through Pictures

Affirming Love

***

Laurie's Story

"Feast on Affirmation"

Our family was eating supper, and my four-year-old son Sam was eager to tell his father about the science class he had taken that morning. Sam loved the class. We enjoyed listening to his stories, and I could see pride in Steve's eyes as he happily affirmed Sam and praised him for his accomplishments.

I listened to all this, and a few social graces that Sam needed to learn came to mind. You see, this class was Sam's first school experience. So, I got to thinking that maybe Steve and I could give Sam a few pointers. I was getting ready to mention some of these issues when it dawned on me that we should feast on affirmation, especially during supper. I knew that I would quell Sam's enthusiasm if I offered my suggestions, and I just couldn't kill his spirit by ending the meal with criticism. So, I let the socialization issues go. I made a choice that evening. Our supper could have ended in criticism, but it didn't. We shared a heathy helping of affirmation instead.

***

Heavenly Hint

"Every day, as long as this today lasts, keep encouraging (affirming) one another..."
Hebrews 3:13

***
Reflection

The fifth commandment given by God is, "You shall not murder." Just as it is not acceptable to kill the physical body, neither is it acceptable to kill the spirit. We remind mothers that their children have not yet fully matured, and their youthful spirit is something to hold dear. Sometimes, our children's concerns may seem unimportant because we have grown past them, but they are always important to our children as they are still growing and learning. As Saint Teresa of Calcutta wisely advised, "Spread love everywhere you go: first of all in your own house. Give love to your children… Be the living expression of God's kindness; kindness in your face, kindness in your eyes, kindness in your smile, kindness in your warm greeting." Our children's spirits are precious. We should nurture them, for while nurturing a child, we are surely nurturing God Himself.

In God's love for us, He repeatedly affirms us in His holy word. God does this because He is our Father, and He loves us. Affirmation is an effective way to demonstrate this love. It recognizes that God created us in His image, and as it says in Psalm 139:14, we were "fearfully and wonderfully made." Yes, we were made perfectly by God; however, we will never remain perfect because of the fallen world. God knows this and affirms us as a way to show He loves us despite our failings. Laurie recognized this in the above story. She decided to model God's affirming love and hold off correcting Sam. That decision allowed Sam to take pride in himself and feel the affirming love of his father.

As moms, we need to imitate God's affirming and encouraging love. We have the daunting power to tear down or to build up our children's spirits. As God's holy word tells us in Proverbs 18:21, "Death and life are in the gift of the tongue, those who indulge it must eat the fruit it yields." Laurie could have used her tongue to criticize Sam and would have yielded the fruit of killing Sam's spirit at that moment. In that case, supper would have ended in sorrow rather than joy.

So, may we, as the heart of the home, look for those affirming moments and encourage our children because those are what will build up our children's spirits. When we look into the eyes of our children, we are indeed looking into the eyes of God. Is our household of faith prepared for such a gift? If the answer is yes, let us daily look for ways to affirm our children with loving hearts and Godly tongues, consistently pursuing the best in them.

***

Homework from Heaven

"Positive Placemats"

Materials:
- 11"x14" construction paper
- Thin markers
- Glue

What to Do:
1. To help acknowledge our children's gifts, gather the family together for the following activity.
2. Get a white 11"x14" piece of construction paper to be used as a placemat.
3. Have every person select a heart. (Create the hearts in advance. Use varying colors, staying within the size of your hand).
4. Glue the heart in the very center of the paper. Have different colored thin markers in a basket available for all.
5. Have everyone write on a heart, "God made me with special gifts."
6. Next, a parent sets the timer for a minute and says, "Go." Everyone moves one place to the right and then writes one special gift that they appreciate about that particular family member. For example, I love Jonathan's tender heart; or I

love Maggie's gentle spirit. When the timer goes off, everyone moves one place to the right. Write an affirmation to that member of the family. Keep doing the same until you return to your original spot.
7. Laminate the placemats and use them when you feast as a family.

***

Prayerful Pause

*Dear Father,
Nudge me to use affirmations
when that is what my child needs.
Amen.*

***
Memos to Me

***
Pondering through Pictures

An Attitude of Gratitude

***

Laurie's Story
"Be Mindful of What You Wish For"

One Saturday, our family had been vegging out watching T.V. for far too long. Suddenly, Steve got up and turned it off, saying, "Enough's enough!" Then, he told the kids that he wanted them to do something together. So, he gave them our camcorder and challenged them to make a video. They loved the idea and told Steve and me to stay in the house until they called us because they wanted it to be a surprise. Then, they eagerly ran outside to work on it. When they finished, we returned to the TV to watch it. Steve and I giggled throughout the video and had a great time watching our children's creativity. They were very entertaining, and we were proud of what they'd done and let them know it. To our surprise, the kids told us it was our turn to make a video for them. So off we went.

After brainstorming some different ideas, we chose a theme for our video. We decided we wanted wealth, and the time to do whatever we wanted. So, at the start of the video, we had a conversation about selling our children for the millions we knew they were worth. We decided to do it. Now, as a millionaire, Steve wouldn't have to work anymore, and with the kids gone, neither would I. We became instantly rich with all kinds of time on our hands.

We demonstrated our newfound wealth by gathering a bunch of Monopoly™ money and putting it in our safe. Now, we could do anything we wanted. Steve and I started shouting, "No, kids! Wow, now we can do anything we want. Look at all the stuff the kids play with." Steve mischievously grinned at me saying, "Haha, now it's ours. What do you want to do first?" I answered, "Jump for joy! - on the trampoline of course." We also tried out the kids' Ripstiks™, played their video games, and ate all the ice cream by ourselves. But the outcome surprised us.

    The trampoline jumping had to stop almost before it started because, after eight children, my bladder wasn't what it used to be. There goes the joy. The Ripstik™ riding also came to an abrupt halt when Steve went crashing to the ground and twisted his knee. So, I helped Steve hobble into the house and suggested we sit down and play video games while he iced his injury. While I was getting the ice pack out of the freezer, I spotted two gallons of ice cream, so I grabbed them and a couple of spoons. I thought our eyes couldn't have been bigger than our stomachs, but I was wrong. While we gorged on ice cream, the games soaked up all our time. Minutes turned into days and days turned into weeks. At this point, we decided we had better go jogging because reality hit - Our stomachs had expanded, and our clothes no longer fit. Our jog slowed to speed walking which morphed into plodding along until we finally fell to our knees crawling to the front lawn where we collapsed like starfish on the grass.

    The next day, we decided to give Frisbee™ a go. However, we didn't realize how exhausting it was without eight other people running for the disc too. Whew! After tossing a few back and forth, Steve felt ambitious and made a jump for the Frisbee™, but as it headed toward the pool, Steve did too. In he went! As I ran over to save Steve, he popped out of the water and startled me, making me fall in. I looked at Steve and said, "We're pathetic! Look at us - we own a trampoline that we can't jump on, we have Ripsticks™ that we can't stay on, and we don't even fit in our clothes anymore because of too much gaming and goodies." Steve looked at me and said, "We're all washed up! This wasn't worth it." I nodded, saying, "Wealth and time for us aren't everything they're cracked up to be. - I miss the kids."

"I do too."

"I thought it would be so great to finally have the place to ourselves and be able to do whatever we wanted."

"I did too, but I guess this just isn't the life for us. Let's give the money back."

"Yeah, I'd work my fingers to the bone if I could only hug my children one more time."

"I don't care if I have to work day and night to make ends meet. I want my kids back." Immediately we got in the car to return the money. After the exchange, we were told that the kids would be home when we got there. So, we plodded along as quickly as we could to the car and dashed home. Sure enough, when we pulled up, the kids came running out of the house, pointing and giggling at the state we were in. We just stood there with our arms opened wide - we knew they'd make it to us - they're kids after all! The Robbins' nest was back in all its glory!

***

Heavenly Hint

"Rejoice always...
give thanks in all circumstances;
for this is the will of God..."
1 Thessalonians 5:16,18

***

Reflection

God's sixth commandment is, "You shall not commit adultery." We, of course, recognize that it is never acceptable to commit adultery. However, the principle behind adultery is breaking down relationships. Remember what the Heavenly Hint says, "Rejoice always… give thanks in all circumstances; for this is the will of God…" Relationships break down when people stop appreciating the family and friends God has put in their lives. God has put our children into our lives for a reason. Sometimes, motherhood can feel monotonous or trying, and moms desire more freedom. To avoid feeling resentment, mothers need to stay focused on being thankful and content for the people God has already given them.

In the video mentioned in Laurie's story, Steve and Laurie forgot to pray in thanksgiving for the eight amazing people God sent their way. Instead of thanking God for their eight blessings, Steve and Laurie focused on being inconvenienced. They turned their heads to the desire for time and money. By lamenting about their lack of time and money, Laurie and Steve not only broke down their relationship with their children – they completely severed it. However, by the end of the video, Steve and Laurie discovered they wanted their wonderful life back because they recognized their children were their real treasures. Steve and Laurie no longer fantasized about a life of wealth and leisure.

When we live a life of gratitude, there is no need for more freedom or resentment because we are thankful for our children and content with our lives. As our sixteenth president, Abraham Lincoln, once said, "We can complain because rose bushes have thorns, or we can rejoice because thorn bushes have roses." Moms, let us be happy and thank God for what He has given us, especially for each of our children and the gift that they are to us.

***

Homework from Heaven

"Making Family Videos"/ "Thank You Notes"

What to Do: "Making Family Videos"
1. Follow Steve and Laurie's example by having both the parents and the children make fun family videos.
2. Encourage some of the videos to demonstrate an attitude of gratitude.

***

What to Do: "Thank You Notes"
1. Let your children see you write thank you notes when you receive a gift or a show of kindness from family or friends. It is an excellent way to model thankfulness to your children.
2. When your children receive a gift, teach/encourage them to write a thank you note and mail it. Writing thank you notes helps to mold grateful hearts.

***

Prayerful Pause

Dear Father,
Please help us to be happy
with what You've given us and to
live our lives with grateful hearts.
Amen.

***
Memos to Me

_____
_____
_____
_____
_____
_____
_____

***
Pondering through Pictures

Sleep Sweet

***

Laurie's Story

"The Crawler"

Mary has never been a good sleeper. One day, I asked her why. She explained, "My whole life, I've called myself a conscious sleeper because part of my brain was in light sleep, but another part of my brain was aware that I was lying in my bed. This conscious awareness made nights go on forever, resulting in me never feeling fully rested.

During one of my sister's visits from Oregon, she told me I stopped breathing at night. She further said that the previous night she observed me not breathing, but rather than waking me, she decided to time how long I stopped breathing. After about a minute, she said I gasped for air. When I told Aaron this, he decided to perform the same experiment. He, too, observed that I stopped breathing for about a minute, and then gasped for air.

So, at my next physical, I told my doctor what the two of them did. He followed up with a surprising question, "Don't they love you?" Honest to Pete, that was his question. I laughed with him. He recommended that I participate in a sleep study. I did, and the study revealed that I stopped breathing frequently and that my oxygen saturation dropped to sixty-eight percent. They explained that when someone's oxygen saturation drops below ninety-two percent, it is a cause for concern. It was safe to say that we were all concerned. The solution was for me to get a Continuous Positive Airway Pressure machine or CPAP."

The CPAP is quite a contraption. It has a mask that covers Mary's nose with a tube connected to it. The other end of the tube attaches to the CPAP machine itself. The machine blows air through the tube and into the mask, keeping Mary breathing steadily. Now, her tongue stays forward. Without the machine, her tongue falls back and blocks her airway. The CPAP allows Mary to sleep deeply. She laughed and told me, "Now, I sleep so soundly that when someone touches me or stands over me, it wakes me with a start, and I scream. It scares my family. So, at times, Aaron will wake me by turning off the CPAP, which cuts off my air supply and wakes me up." However, Mary neglected to tell me that she wakes up in a panic, with a feeling of being suffocated, and that Aaron only does this on the rare occasion that he is struggling to wake her, and they are in a time crunch.

Now that you know the background, I can tell you what happened one time when I came up to spend the night at Mary's house. We were doing something important early the next morning, but what that was escapes me. When morning came, I awoke to my alarm and peeked in on Mary, who was still sound asleep, with her alarm blaring.

At this point, I realized that I would have to wake her up because she was slow to rise, and I didn't want us to get into a time crunch. At that moment, I recalled Mary telling me how much it startles her when people stand over her to wake her up. I didn't want to do that to her, so I began thinking of an alternative. Then, it dawned on me that sometimes Aaron turns off her CPAP to wake her up. So, remembering that it only takes standing over Mary to startle her, I decided to crawl on my hands and knees, so she wouldn't see me coming.

I got to the bedside stand that held Mary's CPAP and gingerly reached up and turned it off. Then, I backed out quietly on all fours and waited outside the bedroom door to see what would happen. I watched Mary gasp for air, jerk up, and then throw off her mask and look around to see what had happened. She got up, panicked as she stumbled toward me into the hallway, discombobulated and half asleep. Clearly, I had failed at my attempt not to startle her. When she saw me, Mary asked me, "Is the electricity out?"

"No."

"Did you turn off my machine?"

"Yes."

"Why?"

"Because that's what Aaron does to wake you up," and clapping with awkward glee, I continued, "That's a good thing, right!?"

"If you want to suffocate me!" Mary said with big eyes. Then, Mary looked at me quizzically and asked, "How did you get my CPAP turned off without waking me?" I proceeded to explain to Mary how I had crawled on the floor to get to her CPAP unobtrusively. But before I could finish my story, we were both laughing so hard that, ironically, Mary needed to get her inhaler to breathe.

***

Heavenly Hint

"My child, do not let these escape from your sight: sound wisdom and prudence...If you sit down, you will not be afraid; when you lie down, your sleep will be sweet."
Proverbs 3:21,24

***

Reflection

"You shall not steal" is the seventh commandment. Again, let us look at the principle behind stealing. In a homily at church, a priest once talked about stealing uniquely. He began by sharing that in twenty-four hours, eight hours should be given to work, eight hours given to family life, and eight hours to sleep. God made it day and night for a reason. Be careful not to "steal" time from God's intended plan. God made the night so that we could shut down and rest.

It can sometimes be tempting to stay up late and try to

finish what we planned to accomplish that day, but that time did not allow for. A mom's day can have unexpected twists and turns that put a dent in her plans. Staying up late to make up for the lost time to finish those plans may seem like a good idea, but it is not always prudent. It makes for a cranky mom the next day. Mary can attest to this. Before using her CPAP, Mary never felt fully on top of her game. She was constantly fatigued. Sleep is vital because the proper amount of sleep keeps us alert and allows us to make better decisions. "Our hearts were made for You, O Lord, and they are restless until they rest in you," said Saint Augustine. God gently recharges us. This peaceful time with Him will enable the next sixteen hours to be productive in achieving His will. Once refreshed, we are better able to give our children the best versions of ourselves.

As moms, there are times when our minds are so active that it makes it more difficult to fall asleep. We can get focused on the problems of the day or on those that are looming. Saint Teresa Benedicta of the Cross tells us, "...Just take everything exactly as it is, put it in God's hands and leave it with Him. Then you will be able to rest in Him - really rest - and start the next day, as a new life." Trust in God to take care of tomorrow - He always does!

***

Homework from Heaven

"Drop Everything"

What to Do:

Set an alarm at an established time to remind you to drop everything and start your bedtime routine. Make sure you give yourself enough time to complete your routine and fall asleep, thus ensuring you get eight hours of rest.

***
Prayerful Pause

*Dear Father,
Help us to model and teach our children the importance of a good night's sleep. For when we rest in You, we are better prepared to be the best version of ourselves.
Amen.*

***
Memos to Me

_____
_____
_____
_____
_____
_____
_____
_____

***
Pondering through Pictures

Let Us Respond

***

Mary's Memory
"Hold Your Tongue"

One evening at the supper table, we were having a rough go of it. My daughter, Maggie, was four or five years old at the time and had a bad attitude. Every time my daughter, Kathleen, said something, Maggie would respond in a snarky manner by talking over her or insulting her. I was so irritated by the middle of supper that I told her, "Maggie, you haven't said one kind thing to your sister, so if you can't say something nice, then just hold your tongue." Maggie gave me a puzzled look, stuck out her tongue, and held it between her thumb and pointer finger while lisping, "How long do I have to hold it?"

***

Heavenly Hint

*"Let the words of my mouth
and the meditation of my heart
be acceptable to you, O Lord..."*
Psalm 19:14

***

Reflection

The eighth commandment God gave us is, "You shall not bear false witness against your neighbor." Typically, this means not saying something untrue about another person. Most people are taught not to bear false witness against their neighbor, but are they taught to look for ways to build them up? We ask this question because Scripture tells us in Ephesians 4:29, "Let no evil talk come out of your mouths, but only what is useful for building up, as there is need, so that your words may give grace to those who hear." In Mary's memory above, Maggie was not being evil to her sister, but she certainly was not building her up either. So, Mary asked her to hold her tongue. Kathleen did not react to her sister's interruptions by saying hurtful or angry things back. She just fell silent in the moments of Maggie's impulsive words, and once Maggie settled, she would try again.

Two people held their tongues that night. One in kindness, and the other, because she was learning a lesson about what it meant to be kind. The expression "hold your tongue" is another way to say we will choose to respond rather than react.

Teaching our children when to hold their tongues promotes harmony and kind people. Teaching our children that their words matter is essential because words can either hurt or help people. And that is why we need to teach our children to think before they speak. Philippians 4:8 tells us, "Finally, beloved, whatever is true, whatever is honorable, whatever is just, whatever is pure, whatever is pleasing, whatever is commendable, if there is any excellence and if there is anything worthy of praise, think about these things." This Scripture quote is sound because when our minds think good things, our tongues speak good things.

Mothers, this is important for us to remember as well. We need to be mindful of how we react to the things our children say and do. If we can keep our minds filled with virtuous thoughts, we can remain composed when a problematic situation arises with our children. In this way, we limit reacting spontaneously and emotionally, and instead, we are already in a place to prayerfully and thoughtfully respond to the situation. Responding and reacting are not the same thing. When we pause, we give ourselves the chance to remain composed rather than have a knee-jerk reaction. We encourage mothers to take that pause. It will allow them to use God's grace to help them respond with love.

As moms, we want our responses to build a solid bridge between our children and us. As we take the time to respond to our children prayerfully and thoughtfully in love, we are, little by little, building a solid bridge upon which our children feel safe to walk toward us and be in a relationship with us. Suppose we indulge in merely reacting to our children's behavior or desires. In that case, the bridge becomes unstable, and our children will become uncertain about whether they want to risk crossing it or not because they might get hurt. Responding promotes the Scripture above, for we use our words to build up our children by considering their needs. With intention, we choose words that benefit our children as they listen.

Laurie demonstrates this beautifully with her children. When her children come to her and ask for something, and her answer is no, sometimes they push back, as children often do. When necessary, she holds her ground. Other times, she listens to their reasons for wanting a yes response rather than reacting to their pushback. Then, she often responds with, "Let me think about it." This response allows time for Laurie to prayerfully and thoughtfully reconsider her decision. It may not change, which may aggravate her children, but they also know that they were listened to, and Laurie maintained her integrity by being the best version of herself.

Throughout our writing here, we have chosen not only to thoughtfully but to also prayerfully respond. That is because when we pray, even if for a moment, we allow God's grace to guide our decisions. God's grace helps us to respond with love. When we habitually let God guide us, it will become easier and easier to hold our tongues.

***

Homework from Heaven

"Whatever"

Materials:
- Large poster boards
- Bible
- Sharpies™, paint, glitter, etc.

What to Do:

The word whatever has become a word to use dismissively. When people get unhappy about what is said to them, they might say, "Whatever" rudely and walk away. If this happens in Mary's home, she typically whips out three of the phrases from Philippians 4:8, whichever fits the situation best. Here is the scripture again, "Finally, beloved, whatever is true, whatever is honorable, whatever is just, whatever is pure, whatever is pleasing, whatever is commendable, if there is any excellence and if there is anything worthy of praise, think about these things." It didn't take her children long to stop the disrespectful bad habit.

1. Have your child write the Scripture verse Philippians 4:8 on the poster board and decorate it however they wish.
2. Frame it and then hang it somewhere in your house.

***

Prayerful Pause

*Dear Father,
Please strengthen our children's resolve to think before they speak, and please help us to do the same.
Amen.*

***
Memos to Me

_____
_____
_____
_____
_____
_____
_____

***
Pondering through Pictures

Sharing Gifts

***

Mary's Memory

"Be Yourself"

I was a teacher before I had children. I did not get my own classroom right out of college, so I spent a year subbing. With all the different classrooms I taught in, I created a three-ring binder of all the procedures and ideas I especially liked so I could implement them once I got my own classroom.

When I became a mom, I was determined to do the same thing. While I did not make a three-ring binder, I watched other moms and how they interacted with their children. I tried to implement what I liked, but it became overwhelming because I was so busy trying the things that worked for other moms that I was losing myself. I was thinking about how to be a mom rather than just being a mom and staying true to myself. Over time, I learned that I could only take what I thought were the best ideas from other moms, allowing me to keep the best of myself.

***
Heavenly Hint

*"Now there are varieties of gifts,
but the same Spirit; and there are varieties
of services, but the same Lord; and there
are varieties of activities, but it is the
same God who activates
all of them in everyone."
1 Corinthians 12:4-6*

***
Reflection

God's ninth commandment is, "You shall not covet your neighbor's wife..." To look at this from a mother's perspective, let us discern whether or not we covet another mother's gifts. Every woman has God-given abilities. Moms recognize God's gifts in each other. Mary tried taking advantage of this in her above memory. However, some skills simply cannot be emulated or are too foreign to a person's personality. Mary experienced this directly when she tried to implement the characteristics she admired in other mothers. She discovered that imitation only works in moderation. She determined that God had given her gifts, too, and that she needed to be true to her abilities as well. Galatians 6:4 supports this, "But everyone is to examine his own achievements... not comparing them with anybody else's."

Each of us has abilities other moms would appreciate us sharing with their children. The keyword is to share. [4]In Matthew Kelly's book, Rediscovering the Saints, he reminds his readers that, "We each have a God-given need to belong to a community based on love for one another, where we can each contribute according to our gifts and abilities, and where we can be seen and known for who we really are..." (Kelly 55). Let us allow God to breathe life into our children through the love and talents of other moms. Moms, we can seek out friendships with mothers that we admire, acknowledge that we too do admirable things, and also be prepared to share what others see in us. For as Saint Teresa of Calcutta tells us, "What I can do, you cannot. What you can do, I cannot. But together, we can do something beautiful for God."

***

Homework from Heaven
"Friends in Fun"/ "Friends in Faith"

What to Do: "Friends in Fun"
1. Choose something you enjoy doing with your children and invite another mom and her children to participate in the activity with you. Maybe you can make it a routine and take turns.
2. Why not invite other moms to make it a fun moms' group?

***

What to Do: "Friends in Faith"
1. Think about making an effort once or twice a month to invite a family to your home to share faith and friendship.
2. Make sure you include faith-related activities during the visit that everyone can enjoy together, and don't forget to include some good old-fashioned fun. Here are some examples:

    a. Make ornaments at Christmas and give them to residents in nursing homes.
    b. Make rosaries and donate them. Ask your church who needs them the most.
    c. Play board games or card games for all ages. Go

outside and play badminton, croquet, or some other family-friendly game.
d. There are all kinds of ideas. Brainstorm together and have fun with it!

***

Prayerful Pause

Dear Father,
Thank You for the gifts You have given each mother. May we share them while building holy friendships.
Amen.

***
Memos to Me

_____
_____
_____
_____
_____
_____
_____
_____

***
Pondering through Pictures

People Come First

***

Laurie's Story

"The Mission Changed"

We had gone up to Mary's for a visit one hot summer day. Our boys were playing in the backyard. They brought some rocks inside and put them down on Mary's glass table. The boys were on a mission because Patrick had recently gotten a rock polisher. They thought these rocks could be ones to polish. After a couple of minutes, Mary asked the boys to take the rocks back outside, explaining that her mom had given her the glass table and she liked it because it came from her childhood home. The boys happily took the rocks outside.

Apparently, Sam's and Patrick's mission had changed because Sam came in carrying one big rock. "Sam - don't!" Too late, the rock shattered the table. Mary was in the kitchen and hollered, "What was that?" Silence - awkward silence! Mary rounded the corner, and Sam, Patrick, and I all looked at her wide-eyed. I was afraid Mary was going to be mad. Mary looked at me, and I said, "Sam broke the glass table." To my surprise, Mary answered, "Don't worry, Sam, people are always more important than things."

***

Heavenly Hint

"We brought nothing into the world, and we can take nothing out of it..."
1 Timothy 6:7

***
Reflection

"You shall not covet your neighbor's house... or anything that belongs to your neighbor." is God's tenth commandment. Mothers, what is critical in this commandment is that we teach our children that people come first. Take Laurie's story, for example. Sam accidentally broke Mary's glass table. That table had special memories associated with it, and it was important to Mary. Still, Mary made sure that Sam and Laurie both knew that they were more important when she said, "People are always more important than things." Let us refer back to the Heavenly Hint, "We brought nothing into the world and we can take nothing out of it." If we cannot take anything out of the world, why should we put anything before another person? To throw a little Star Trek in, "It is not logical."

Moms, our children need to know that people are always more important than things. As Pope Francis eloquently reminds us, "Things have a price and can be for sale, but people have a dignity that is priceless and worth far more than things." We need to teach this to our children because no amount of work will bring in enough money to buy them happiness. We cannot risk the possibility of allowing our children to believe that things will bring them more joy than a loving relationship with God or the family and friends He puts in their lives.

***
Homework from Heaven
"Cracked, Chipped, or Broken"

What to Do:

When Mary's mom would find something broken in the house, she would sometimes quip, "I don't own anything that hasn't been cracked, chipped, or broken!" Instead of getting aggravated when something is accidentally damaged or ruined, let us remind ourselves and our children that people are always more important than things in hopes that it becomes our natural response, because people are indeed more precious than things.

***

Prayerful Pause

Dear Father,
May we both model and teach our children that people are the priority and will always be more important than things.
Amen.

***
Memos to Me

***
Pondering through Pictures

God the Son

***

*"For those who love,
nothing is too difficult,
especially when it is done for the love of
our Lord Jesus Christ."*
Saint Ignatius

Pardon Me

***

Laurie's Story

"The Gift of a Mum"

My family was still living in Nebraska that summer. We had just returned home from a vacation to Washington State. With Mom trying to unpack, we were getting underfoot, so she finally yielded to our numerous requests to ride our bikes to the park. We were surprised when Mom said yes because she rarely allowed such a privilege. We gathered our things quickly before she changed her mind. Then it was off to the park - we were thrilled to embark on a new adventure together. Little did we know the adventure would take place on the home front that day.

After we took off, Mom went into the back bedroom to put my little sister Stephanie down for her nap. Mom returned to the family room to continue unpacking. As Mom unpacked a new basket she had brought back from the trip, she went to hang it above the snack bar. As she did this, she heard a noise coming from the back bedroom and thought she should check on Stephanie. While checking in on my sister, Mom heard a big swishing sound, followed by a loud thud. Mom dashed back to the family room and cautiously entered a room now filled with smoke. Behind the snack bar, she saw a crack in the mirror tile. Upon looking more closely, she couldn't tell what had happened, so she immediately called the sheriff.

The sheriff figured it was just some kids playing with a BB gun, but Mom thought it was more serious than that and urged the sheriff to come check it out for himself. When the sheriff arrived, he inspected the family room to determine what had happened. He went over to the mirror for a closer look. Then, the sheriff took out his knife and dug out the culprit - a large, smashed deer bullet. The bullet had passed through the twenty-foot room and had lodged in the mirror behind the bar. It hit the mirror just inches from where Mom had been hanging the basket.

A couple of days later, my mom was out planting mums in the garden when the sheriff arrived with a neighbor and his two sons. The sheriff explained that the boys had been playing with their father's deer rifle when it unexpectedly fired. The sheriff brought the boys over to see the consequences of their actions. Mom explained how the bullet could have killed her. The younger boy stood trembling as he stared at the hole in the mirror. Mom told the sheriff that she would not press charges, and while the sheriff talked with the boys' father about keeping the gun and bullets locked up, his youngest son began to cry. Mom no longer saw a child that could have killed her or one of her children. Instead, she saw a child filled with fear and remorse for what he had done but did not know how to make it right again. God's Spirit overcame my mother, filling her with compassion and forgiveness. Mom offered the boy one of her mums. The boy hugged Mom. My mom patterned herself after Jesus that day. She was sympathetic and loving toward her neighbor and forgave him as readily as Jesus forgives us.

***
Heavenly Hint

"Bear with one another; forgive each other if one of you has a complaint against another. The Lord has forgiven you; now you must do the same."
Colossians 3:13

***
Reflection

What does it mean to forgive someone? To forgive someone means to have a heart willing to give up our right to restitution and, instead, forgive the wrong done to us. This kind of forgiveness is demonstrated in Laurie's story above. The younger boy was visibly shaken and clearly sorry, and Laurie's mom could see that. And while she had every right to press charges or yell at the boys and berate the dad for being irresponsible, she simply chose to forgive them. Jesus did this as He was dying on the cross, for He had every right to ask His Father for restitution, but instead, He asked His Father to forgive the wrong done to Him.

So how do we teach our children the importance of forgiveness? We follow Jesus' example for "God's heart is more gentle than the Virgin's first kiss upon the Christ. And God's forgiveness to all, to any thought or act, is more certain than our own being." says Saint Catherine of Siena. Answering God's call to be Christlike to our children will take listening to Jesus in our hearts and allowing His love and forgiveness to pour from us to our children.

As our children are learning to accept us with all our imperfections, should not we accept our children with all of their imperfections as well? Therein lies the importance of teaching our children forgiveness, as none of us are perfect. There is healing in learning to ask, "Will you forgive me?" and to offer the words, "Yes, I forgive you." Healing occurs when these words are spoken because both parties will need to humble themselves. The offender, in having to admit wrongdoing, and the offended, in having to pardon.

As mothers, we all know it is difficult to be everything we should be for our children. When we fall short and our children bear the brunt, we can grasp the opportunity to reconcile with our children. Saying I'm sorry is essential, but asking, "Will you forgive me?" provides so much more because it demonstrates that we hold our children and our relationship with them dear. We can look our children in the eyes with love and say, "I'm sorry. Will you forgive me?" This question invites our children to the healing power of Jesus by allowing them to respond, "Yes, I forgive you" freely. Why does this act of love show our children that we hold our relationship with them dear? Because it turns the tables and makes us vulnerable to them, for they may not be ready to forgive us, and we will need to accept that and give their hearts some time to get there.

Respecting our children in this way is essential because when we look into their eyes, we look into the eyes of God. In James 4:10, it states, "Humble yourselves before the Lord and He will lift you up." For it is in this act of humility that our children have the opportunity to forgive, and we have the chance to be forgiven. The Lord can uplift us in forgiveness, and we will both find Jesus' peace.

Reconciliation needs to extend to all of our family members, not just between mothers and their children. The words "I'm sorry" need to be used carefully. Before someone says they are sorry, it is important they take time to reflect on whether they will change their behavior. It is also important they take time to determine whether or not they are just saying "I'm sorry" to end the conflict because they know they will never truly lose family, for family sticks together for life.

If the offender does not reflect on their behavior and come to a willingness to change first and simply says a quick, I'm sorry, they risk the offended not believing in their apology. Forgiveness can be hard when a person does not believe in an apology's sincerity. This is why Mary taught her children when they were young that it is difficult for people to think that we are sincerely sorry if we hurt them over and over again in the same way. She would tell her children, "With 'I'm sorry' comes change." She did this so that her children would experience genuine forgiveness. A person can readily extend forgiveness to all people when they experience genuine forgiveness themselves, knowing the peace and tranquility it brings.

Siblings quarrel, fathers and sons disagree, and husbands and wives squabble, but the family who commits to forgiving each other and changing their behavior will ultimately live in a peaceful home. This is the healing power of forgiveness. Healing takes place when we stay open to Jesus' compassion and forgiveness, for it makes room for us to forgive as readily as Laurie's mom did.

***

Homework from Heaven

"How Do We Fix This?"

What to Do:

Let's say you catch your child in the act of taking a cookie from the cookie jar without permission. You take the cookie away from the child, making them angry. You're upset and disappointed in your child, and your child is upset that their cookie is gone. Rather than simply punishing your child for disobeying, consider talking to them about the situation. An excellent way to start is to sit with them and ask, "What just happened?" Once you and your child agree about what happened, the next question would be, "How do we fix this?" Listen to your child's answers and respond accordingly. Then navigate the conversation toward forgiveness by asking, "You just upset me, and my response just upset you, so how do we fix this?" The goal here would be to get to, "I'm sorry, will you forgive me?" and hear back, "Yes, I forgive you."

Continue these kinds of conversations as your children get older. Grow with them by keeping the conversations age appropriate.

***

Prayerful Pause

*Dear Savior,
May we accept Your healing power in our lives so that Your love and forgiveness flow freely in our households of faith.
Amen.*

***
Memos to Me

_____

_____

_____

_____

_____

_____

_____

***
Pondering through Pictures

Mended Hearts

***

Mary's Memory

"Mom Forgave Me"

One day when Mom was terminally ill, I was quietly watching her. She was reading a book as she so often did. It helped her to fill the long hours. At this point, she could no longer get around without help and required a great deal of care. A feeling of unworthiness came over me. Here was this woman who loved me so much, and it hit me that I was not always as good to her as she certainly deserved. A feeling of contrition fell over my heart in that moment. So, I asked her forgiveness for all the times I had hurt her throughout my life. Mom looked at me with a gentle smile. Her answer was simple, "Isn't that just a part of growing up, Honey?" I felt God's faithful love pouring over me as I looked into Mom's eyes. It was then I realized in a new way that it would not have mattered what I did. Mom would have loved me with open arms.

***

Heavenly Hint

"Be kind to one another, tenderhearted, forgiving one another, as God in Christ has forgiven you."
Ephesians 4:32

***
Reflection

As we mature and come to appreciate all the gracious gifts and blessings from God, we grow in love and gratitude for Jesus Christ, our Savior. While this brings us great happiness and contentment, our sins can bring us sorrow and regret. We understand more fully the hurt we have caused others and the pain we have caused our friend Jesus, who has been nothing but good to us. This sorrow can be thought of as a blessing, for it can drive us to improve ourselves by making better choices.

Mary's memory above is bittersweet - bitter for the sin but sweet for the blessing of forgiveness that came out of it. As Mary sat quietly and watched her mom read, contrition overcame her for the times she had hurt her mom. She understood at that moment that her mom deserved better, which is why when her mom said, "Isn't that just a part of growing up, Honey?" it made an impression on Mary. Mary's mom's forgiveness came as quickly as a blink of an eye. She emulated what Jesus told us from the cross in Luke 23:34, "Father, forgive them; for they do not know what they are doing." Mary's mom forgave Mary because she, like Jesus, understood that Mary did not always know her words and actions were hurtful.

Comforted by her mom's unfailing love and mercy, Mary understood forgiveness in a new way, and it mended her heart that day. This experience allowed Mary to grow from the sorrow she was experiencing. It taught her that her children would hurt her, but it would just be a part of them growing up and learning how to maneuver life. So, moms, remember sometimes when our children hurt us, it is not with intention. This is especially true in the innocence of our younger children. They do not always understand that they are being hurtful because they have not yet learned it. It is just part of growing up.

In the story above, Mary knew that her mom was dying and did not have long for this world. As she remembered her life with her mom, a quote from an anonymous author came to mind. "We spend years wishing our parents would get off our backs, only to realize that they are the only ones who ever really had our backs." Mary would add today that when they have gone to heaven, we wish we could have them back.

***

Homework from Heaven

"Forgiveness & Time"

Consider...
1. Keeping in mind that growing up is not easy - be generous in love and ready to forgive in the blink of an eye.
2. Being ever mindful of your choices regarding your parents here on earth. Remember, they put up with your shenanigans for years. Show them gratitude by giving them your time. Perhaps take them to supper, give them flowers, or take them to the movies from time to time.

***

Prayerful Pause

Dearest Jesus,
Help us to forgive as readily as You.
Amen.

***
Memos to Me

_____
_____
_____
_____
_____
_____
_____
_____

***
Pondering through Pictures

Follow Me

***

Laurie's Story

"Happy Trails"
(Beth's Creative Writing Paper)

It was a warm day during our spring vacation, and Dad had taken the day off. He wanted to take us to one of his favorite hiking places called Staircase. Staircase was an uphill hike that looped around a river. So, we packed up, got everybody in the van, and headed out. As usual, we sang along to some of our favorite CDs on the ride up. My favorite was Paul Simon's "Loves Me Like a Rock" because we all really got into it.

When we arrived at the parking lot near the trail's head, we all hit the gag-inducing bathroom. Once everyone was ready, we headed toward the trailhead. Once on the trail, some of us ran ahead but were not allowed to pass Dad, while the little ones fell behind with Mom, who was bringing up the rear. As we went, we came across a big ol' tree that had fallen off to the side of the trail, and everyone took their turn trying to climb across it without falling off. After hanging out for a while, we returned to the trail.

We kept walking and talking and came to a washed-out bridge. So, my dad checked to see how deep the river was and decided we could all get across safely if we worked together. The river was moving pretty quickly, and I was intimidated, so I crawled across it. My younger sisters Rebekah, Hannah, and Sarah had to be carried across.

We continued on the trail until we came to a spot in the river where the water had formed into a "pool" that was still, deep, and begging for swimmers. My older sister, Rose, and I found a big rock and jumped off of it into the pool. When we came out of the pool, we laughed, and I said jokingly, "I think I'm on the verge of hypothermia." Mom and Dad decided we better stay and have a snack before hitting the trail again. However, the local bees agreed that they too needed to snack and came to indulge. Sam, my older brother, started batting them away and, of course, got stung. We attended to him and then hit the trail once more, this time with no stops.

When we finally got back to our van, Dad drove us to the nearby lake to finish the family outing. Once we arrived, we discovered several massive logs floating in the lake. Amy, my oldest sister, and Rose paddled around on a couple of them by using them as boats. Hannah, Sarah, and I used the others as diving boards. Thankfully, the lake was a lot warmer than the river's pool, so we got to enjoy it for quite some time. It was an enjoyable day, one definitely worthy of repeating.

***

Heavenly Hint

"I shall instruct you and teach you the way to go; I shall not take my eyes off you."
Psalm 32:8

***

Reflection

Jesus is always with us, much like He was with His apostles. Recall in scripture when Jesus would come across a person and invite that person to follow Him. Following Jesus meant leaving behind the life they knew to walk with Him, eat with Him, listen to Him, and pray with Him. However, it looks different today because we cannot physically walk with Jesus as His apostles did. Nonetheless, Jesus has chosen us; and invited us to come with Him as well.

As moms, our road of life will have twists and turns, highways and byways, on-ramps and exits, stop signs, yield signs, or even dead ends. That is because we cannot anticipate everything in our own lives, much less our children's lives. Our road is ever before us until the day our heart stops, and we are no longer breathing. We can travel alone and see where that takes us or let Jesus lead and see where He takes us. Traveling the road alone can be bumpy as we will likely take wrong turns or run into dead ends and must turn back. We could sit at a stop sign or find ourselves at a yield sign when we should have hit the highway. Taking the road alone means we maintain control of our lives. The question is, where will that take us when our hearts stop, and we are no longer breathing? Will the road end where we hope to be?

Choosing to follow Jesus on our road of life will still have twists and turns, highways and byways, on-ramps and exits, stop signs, yield signs, or dead ends. The difference is we will not be alone, for in Isaiah 30:21 Scripture tells us, "And when you turn to the right or when you turn to the left, your ears shall hear a word behind you, saying, 'This is the way; walk in it.'" When our road presents us with an opportunity to turn, we need to listen for the "Word behind you" because it is Jesus.

While traveling the road of our life, sometimes Jesus will lead us to a stop sign, forcing us to choose whether to turn left, turn right, or keep going forward. It does not have to mean we are stagnant, for Jesus is with us. While at that stop sign, He might be challenging us, and we will need to listen to His guidance in prayer, being careful not to fall off course. In Laurie's story above, her family found themselves at a stop sign when they came upon the big fallen tree. They stopped, but they were not stagnant. They accepted the challenge and took the time to walk or crawl across, careful not to fall off the tree. Moms, let us look at our stop signs as a challenge given to us by God and accept it with the will to move forward as the Robbins family did in Laurie's Story.

On the other hand, there will be times when we come to a highway on-ramp, and Jesus tells us to get on the highway. We must trust that He will give us the courage to continue driving.

Again, let us turn to Laurie's story. When they unexpectedly came to the washed-out bridge, they trusted Steve to lead them safely through the river, just as we will need to trust Jesus to guide us safely through any unexpected situation on our highway. When we grow weary, He will lead us to the next exit to yield onto a byway and appreciate a slower pace. One more time, we look at Laurie's story. After crossing the river and hiking a bit further, they exited off the trail and yielded onto a byway where they found a pool and appreciated the slower pace.

We are not saying that we should be irresponsible when making plans. It merely means that we need to invite Jesus into those plans and listen to His guidance along the road of life. Proverbs 16:9 tells us this, "The human mind plans the way, but the Lord directs the steps." We all know the importance of calendars and a good plan. That helps us stay sane as we navigate our families' lives. When we allow God to guide us, our actions align with Him. As [5]Matthew Kelly says, "God doesn't stand down the road and call us to catch up. He meets us where we are and leads us step-by-step to who he calls us to become" (Kelly 22). We will not want to hold back once we give ourselves to the love of Jesus. We will bloom, and our road will become more and more beautiful, and we will become more and more holy.

When we choose to follow Jesus, we can walk with determination because we do not have to continually question our next step. With Jesus as our guide, our road will lead us to holiness. Choosing not to follow Jesus leaves us with the option of following the world. The world makes promises to us. Promises of comfort in wealth and material possessions. Promises of comfort in power and control. In contrast, Pope Benedict XVI once said, "The world promises comfort, but you were not made for comfort. You were made for greatness."

Mothers, we were made for greatness, and so were our children. We will find our greatness when we choose to, without reservation, follow Jesus. This way, when the day comes that our heart stops and we are no longer breathing, we will be confident that our road has taken us to heaven, for Psalm 73:23,26 tells us, "Nevertheless I am continually with You; You hold my right hand... My flesh and my heart may fail, but God is the strength of my heart and my portion forever."

***

Homework from Heaven

"Cyber Bible"

What to Do:

One of the best ways to allow Jesus to lead your family is to read His holy word. Here is one way to feed both your family's appetite and faith.

1. Make sure everyone in your family who owns a cell phone brings it with them at supper time. Keep the phones on silent and off the table during supper.
2. After supper, have the most tech-savvy parent explain to the children how to download the same Bible App that you and your husband have chosen.
3. Every night after supper, read from the Bible from the cell phones. Perhaps read that day's Gospel reading or pick a Book of the Bible and read it together a little bit each night.
4. After reading from the Cyber Bible, pray about what you read and have the family share their thoughts. Maybe it applied to something happening in a family member's life.
5. Don't make it a long, drawn-out thing. Keep it to twenty minutes unless the family's interest has spontaneously taken more time.

***
Prayerful Pause

*Dear Jesus,
Take my hand and lead me on the road
You have chosen for me. Empower and
strengthen me as we walk together. Please
make me holy on our journey so we may
live together in heaven.
Amen.*

***
Memos to Me

_____
_____
_____
_____
_____
_____
_____
_____
_____

***
Pondering through Pictures

Be the Body of Christ

***

*"Christ has no body now, but yours.
No hands, no feet on earth, but yours.
Yours are the eyes through which Christ
looks compassion into the world. Yours are
the feet with which Christ walks to do
good. Yours are the hands with which
Christ blesses the world."*
Saint Teresa of Avila

An Invitation to Love & Serve

***

Jesus had a servant's heart. Jesus helped people no matter their circumstances or situation. He desired to help people right where they were and did so. He asks us to do the same by being the Body of Christ to one another. We consider this an invitation from Jesus to love and serve Him. One way to do this is through what Catholics call the Corporal Works of Mercy. They are listed below, and there is one more, to bury the dead. Corporal Works of Mercy are merciful acts that help people in need. At times, these acts will be easy and other times challenging, and that is why it will always require a servant's heart. In the following six chapters, we hope to inspire you to respond to people's needs by modeling and teaching your children the Corporal Works of Mercy. Let us look at the Corporal Works of Mercy with hearts that allow us to be inspired to see them as invitations to love and serve one another.

Corporal Works

***

Feed the hungry

Give drink to the thirsty

Welcome the stranger

Clothe the naked

Visit the sick

Visit the imprisoned

Bury the dead

Feed the Hungry

***

Laurie's Story

"Filling the Cupboards"

One summer, I visited a friend. I had brought along my kids to play with her three children. During our visit, my friend confided that they were struggling to make ends meet and didn't have enough money for groceries, so they had been going to the church's food bank for help. When I got home, I explained the situation to Steve. Together, we went to the grocery store, bought food, and then brought it back to my friend's house. It filled her cupboards and was enough to carry them to the next paycheck. My friend was very grateful and filled with joy at our surprise. Her joy made my heart happy.

***

Heavenly Hint

"Those who are generous are blessed, for they share their bread with the poor."
Proverbs 22:9

***

Reflection

Jesus' first invitation to love and serve is to "Feed the Hungry." In Laurie's story above, Laurie and Steve were the Body of Christ to her friend's family that day, for they recognized that

"Each one of them is Jesus in disguise," as Saint Teresa of Calcutta once said.

Feeding families is critical for their physical health, but feeding their souls is imperative, for in John 6:35 Scripture says, "Jesus answered them: 'I am the Bread of Life. No one who comes to Me will ever hunger...'" Scripture tells us to sustain our children with the "Bread of Life." Jesus is telling us here that just as we cannot physically thrive without the nourishment of food, neither can we spiritually thrive without nourishing ourselves with Him.

When we do not eat, we become physically weak and tired. It is hard to accomplish things as it becomes difficult to concentrate because our focus is on our basic need for food. We simply cannot thrive. This is true spiritually as well. When we separate ourselves from Jesus, our souls become spiritually weak. We are not satisfied, as if something is missing. That missing something is Jesus. Pope John II says, "It is Jesus that you seek when you dream of happiness; He is waiting for you when nothing else you find satisfies you." Without Jesus, we seek satisfaction from this world, leading us down a destructive path. The world cannot provide us with the comfort, love, and hope or promise of something better to come that Jesus gives.

Feeding our physical bodies is not always easy. It takes time and effort. The same is true in our spiritual life. Jesus' call is not always easy. He stretches us by asking us to do things that can take us out of our comfort zone. When we strive to make the world a better place, our soul finds satisfaction in our efforts, for the Lord unites with us. The same is true for our children, but it is necessary to teach them this. We will have to take it in stages, being careful not to overwhelm them, but teach them, nonetheless. Saint Francis of Assisi had it right when he said, "Start by doing what is necessary, then what is possible, and suddenly you are doing the impossible."

As moms, we must be careful not to limit our children, for with Jesus, there are no limits. It is quite the opposite; He will stretch them. Then, they will grow. They will grow in a way that makes them look beyond themselves to a world that needs Jesus alive through them. For example, when Mary was in high school, she took a class called Community Service. Community Service was a class where the students leave the school to volunteer at a placement in the community. Mary was scared to take the class because she lived thirty minutes from her high school and was not familiar with the area. She only drove directly to and from the school each day. She easily got lost and was terrified of ending up in a place where she had no idea how to get back to somewhere familiar. Added to that was the fear of having to put out either her mom or her teacher by calling one of them and asking them to come help her. Mary knew that she would be inconveniencing them by taking them away from their job. Mary's parents knew her fear but encouraged her to take the class anyway.

When it came time to choose from the variety of placements, Mary chose a nursing home because it was the closest placement to the school. She knew that she could get to and from it easily because it was literally one turn from the school and maybe three minutes away if that. Going into the nursing home intimidated Mary. She did not live near any of her grandparents and had limited experience with older people. In the end, Mary was so grateful that she chose the nursing home. Mary's mom and dad stepped back by allowing Jesus to stretch her out of her comfort zone and take the Community Service class. Then, they proudly watched as Mary grew in confidence and allowed Jesus to unite with her as she gave His love to the people in the nursing home. It was a huge blessing in her life as Mary will soon share in an upcoming memory.

Mothers, after we encourage our children to allow Jesus to stretch them beyond their comfort zones, let us then step back and watch what happens, with a heart ever ready to step in if they need our help. In this way, we give them an opportunity to unite with Jesus, the "Bread of Life."

***
Homework from Heaven
"Filling a Need"

What to Do:
Here are some things to help in the spiritual stages of your child's growth. We based them on Saint Francis of Assisi's quote, "Start by doing what is necessary, then what is possible, and suddenly you are doing the impossible." Let's take a look:

1. Necessary Things - start at home:
    a. Clean your room and make your bed.
    b. Pick up toys or your mess around the house.
    c. Remember to smile.
    d. Clear your place from the table and help with the dishes.
    e. Help your brothers and sisters if they need it.
    f. Do your homework.
2. Possible Things:
    a. Take food to the food bank.
    b. Serve in a soup kitchen.
    c. Fill gallon-sized freezer bags with bottled water, protein bars, fruit snacks, and the like. On the outside of the bag, write "God Bless You" with a Sharpie™ pen. Then, take them to a shelter and pass them out to those in need.
    d. Sponsor a child or a family in need who lives outside of the country.
3. Impossible Things:
    a. With Jesus, the sky's the limit!

***
Prayerful Pause

*Dear Jesus,
When we see that others are hungry,
help us find a way to feed them.
Amen.*

***
Memos to Me

_____
_____
_____
_____
_____
_____
_____
_____

***
Pondering through Pictures

Satisfy the Thirsty

***

Laurie's Story

"Rose's Quick Fix"

I used to try hard to drink eight glasses of water a day. But with eight kids, my days often get busy, and drinking water gets away from me. So, I have tried various methods to remind myself to drink water. I tried putting eight rubber bands around my wrist at the start of the day, and every time I drank a cup of water, I would take off one of the bands. This method worked only sporadically because when I was in the car, I'd see the rubber bands but wouldn't have water readily available, or because I would get so busy, I would forget about them altogether. Then, I tried putting the rubber bands on a cup I would carry around. While I managed to drink more water, it still didn't solve the problem if I left the house and didn't have the cup with me. Leaving the house without my cup is easy to do because, with eight kids and many activities to get to, we're usually dashing out the door. Finally, I kept a journal and would tally off each glass of water I drank, but the pen and paper didn't have legs.

My daughter, Rose, saw that I was trying way too hard. So, at Christmas, she found a quick fix for my problem. She gave me a beautiful soft pink water bottle with unique markings of encouragement and a list of each hour of the day. For example, the first line reads, "8 AM - Get Started!" By midday, it reads - "You're Getting Somewhere Now!" And by the end of the day, it reads, "You Did It!" I was so excited and grateful to get this unique gift, and I am delighted that it has worked.

***
Heavenly Hint

*"O God, You are my God,
I seek You, my soul thirsts for You..."*
Psalm 63:1

***
Reflection

Jesus' second invitation to love and serve is to "Give Drink to the Thirsty" or satisfy the thirsty. Water sustains life. God created us with the simple need to drink to stay healthy. A human being can go without food for about three weeks but only survive three to four days without water. It is imperative we diligently teach our children to drink water and start when they are young. One great way to start the habit of drinking water is to do what Rose did for Laurie in the story above. To help our children get enough water, we can buy water bottles for them. Allow them to pick out a water bottle for themselves. Or, go online and let them choose one from a company that will put their name on the bottle. This way, if they take their water bottle to school and lose it, it can be identified. Thankfully, more and more schools will allow, and some even promote, children bringing water bottles to school with them. However, if our child's teacher does not, we could encourage it.

There are long periods throughout the school day when children do not have access to water if they do not have a water bottle. By the end of the school day, they could already be dehydrated. Moms, if we have instilled the habit of drinking plenty of water in our children when they are young, there is a greater chance our children will continue to sustain their bodies with water for a lifetime.

Speaking of school, children's brains have a natural and

unquenchable thirst for knowledge. They will learn whether we teach them or not, so it seems as moms, we should take advantage of this by exposing them to a breadth of things through books. READ, READ, READ for...

> [6]"Children learn to love the sound of language before they even notice the existence of printed words on a page. Reading books aloud to children stimulates their imagination and expands their understanding of the world. It helps them develop language and listening skills and prepares them to understand the written word. When the rhythm and melody of language become a part of a child's life, learning to read will be as natural as learning to walk and talk.
>
> Even after children learn to read by themselves, it's still important for you to read aloud together. By reading stories that are on their interest level, but beyond their reading level, you can stretch young readers' understanding and motivate them to improve their skills."

Reading to children is a fabulous bonding experience and a learning experience. It comes highly recommended by educators as well as us. Even when their children were in middle school, Mary and Aaron loved reading books with them. They would take a series like Narnia, Lord of the Rings, and the controversial Harry Potter. This way, their kids got to experience the stories their peers were talking about, but as parents, Mary and Aaron got to field questions and discuss the issues together. As they read to their children, they would laugh together, or feel angry, and even cry. The time shared was irreplaceable.

We cannot leave out the importance of reading Bible stories. They develop a desire to know more about God. Reading Bible stories from an early age creates a lifetime of familiarity with God, His people, and the stories of God's love and faithfulness.

Beyond that, reading about the saints will help our children to learn that, as Matthew Kelly puts it, [7]"We are capable of so much more than we think... When we have the courage to collaborate with God and pursue our truest self, he lights a fire within us that is so bright and warm, it keeps shining long after our days on earth have come to an end. The lives of the saints have captivated the people of every age for this very reason" (Kelly 9). They will captivate our children too.

Other ways to engage in learning are through community opportunities. When they are interested in a topic, take action. For example, if a child is interested in art, we can take art lessons with them. If a child is interested in music, we can offer them piano lessons as Laurie did for a couple of her kids. Aaron and Steve got involved in their children's athletics, and Aaron became Cub Master for Patrick's Cub Scouts. Finding things to do with our children is not difficult, for children have a natural curiosity and thirst to learn new things. Let their interest lead the way.

Quenching our children's thirst goes past just the physical body and the brain's desire for knowledge. Their souls also thirst. What do their souls thirst for? Jesus tells us in John 4:13-15, "Whoever drinks this water (water from the well) will be thirsty again; but no one who drinks the water that I shall give will ever be thirsty again: the water that I shall give will become a spring of water within, welling up for eternal life." Our souls thirst for Jesus just as our bodies thirst for water. Therefore, it is also imperative that we drink from the water that Jesus gives us to keep our souls healthy.

One way to think of the water that Jesus is referring to is His love. Jesus kept things simple, and one of the simplest of His teachings is that God is love. This water is His love, and He asks us to share it when He tells us in Matthew 22:37-39, "You must love the Lord your God with all your heart, with all your soul, and with all your mind. This is the greatest and the first commandment. The second resembles it: You must love your neighbor as yourself." Loving each other should be easy, but given the fallen world, things complicate it quickly.

God keeps things simple; we muddy it up. Differences of

opinion start eating at us, and before we know it, we are judging each other and, at times, even hurting each other. These behaviors muddy the waters of love and start clogging our hearts, thus stopping the flow of love that feeds our souls. We know this because when we are busy judging others, our focus is not on Jesus' love. As Saint Teresa of Calcutta used to say, "If you judge people, you have no time to love them."

When we lose our focus on the love of Jesus, we begin to thirst for our Lord. Once our souls are thirsty, we are not happy or satisfied, so we seek to quench that thirst. Two great ways to do this are reading the word of God and praying. These keep our hearts and souls fueled with the love of Jesus because they maintain our relationship with Him. We are then better able to do as Jesus commands twofold - first, love God with an "unclogged" heart, and second, give drink to the thirsty by sharing our love.

***

Homework from Heaven

"Thirst for Love" / "Thirst for Knowledge"

What to Do: "Thirst for Love"
1. Give bottled water or, if they take them, water bottles to the local food bank.
2. Every time you take a drink from your water bottle, take the time to ask God to "unclog" your heart and to help you see with new eyes how to love all people more generously.

***

What to Do: "Thirst for Knowledge"
Be attentive to your child's interests and then be prepared to foster them, if possible, together. Here are some ideas:

1. If your child is interested in marine life, take them to the

beach and let them explore the tide pools and marine life.
2. If your child is interested in space, take them to an observatory to see the stars and planets or buy them a telescope.
3. Keep age-appropriate Bibles and Bible storybooks in your house and read and discuss them regularly with your children. Also, keep on hand age-appropriate stories of the lives of the saints.
4. Whatever your child is interested in, always take them to the library to find books about the topic and read about it with them.

***

Prayerful Pause

Sweet Lord,
We thirst in so many ways.
May we be mindful of satisfying
above all, our thirst for You.
Amen.

***
Memos to Me

_____
_____
_____
_____
_____
_____
_____
_____

***
Pondering through Pictures

Welcome the Stranger

***

Laurie's Story

"Poncho"

It was Easter Sunday, and my family and I went to the early morning service. After church, we went to the hall for coffee and donuts. Our family usually sits together while we eat, and then the kids head to the back of the hall to visit and play with their friends. I looked around and noticed a man with a cowboy hat and his dog sitting alone at one of the tables, so I got up and sat with him. I introduced myself, and then he told me his name was Poncho, and his dog's name was Midnight. While Poncho and I visited, my girls would come up and ask questions about Midnight, who was a seeing-eye dog. During the conversation, I decided to ask Poncho, "What are you doing today, Poncho?" Poncho shrugged his shoulders and said, "Nothing."

"Would you want to come over for dinner?"

"I would like that," he responded. So, we settled on picking Poncho and Midnight up at four.

When I arrived at Poncho's apartment, he and Midnight were waiting outside. They both piled in, and we headed back to the house. Dinner was still busily being prepared by Steve and the kids when Poncho and I walked through the door. So, I pulled out a couple of chairs at the dining room table, and Poncho and I sat down. Everybody talked while Steve and the kids created good smells as they worked their magic in the kitchen. It wasn't long before dinner was served.

After dinner, Midnight was ready to go outside and play. It was a beautiful day, so Poncho and I took her out. A few of my girls followed us, and they played fetch with Midnight by tossing balls and Frisbees up in the air for her to catch. The kids got a kick out of Midnight, and she got some serious exercise. After a while, Poncho thought Midnight ought to get some rest since she wasn't used to running around that much. Poncho and I sat down, and before long, we found ourselves entertained by Steve and the kids. We watched them play Frisbee, Bocce ball, and a soccer game where everyone stood in a circle around a big bucket and juggled a soccer ball as they tried to get it in the bucket without letting it touch the ground. I checked with Poncho several times to see if he needed to get home, but Poncho wanted to stay longer.

Finally, Poncho was ready to go, so we got into the van and headed back to his apartment. On the way there, Poncho shared that he had a great time and that seeing all the kids reminded him of years past. It brought a big smile to his face. I told Poncho that we enjoyed having him over and would have to have him over for another visit sometime soon. When we arrived at Poncho's apartment, he continued talking for a little longer before he and Midnight headed inside. Throughout that last conversation, Poncho mentioned that he "enjoyed every minute" of his time with our family, and we enjoyed him in turn!

***

Heavenly Hint

"Welcome one another, therefore, just as Christ has welcomed you, for the glory of God."
Romans 15:7

***

Reflection

"Welcome the Stranger" is Jesus' third invitation to love and serve. In Matthew 8:20, Jesus says, "Foxes have holes, and the birds of the air have nests; but the Son of Man has nowhere to lay

His head." How can we, as moms, provide a pillow for our Savior's head? We remain willing to surrender our hearts and share our homes with someone in need. With this in mind, let us consider our call to love and serve the strangers among us.

A stranger may be a mother's eldest child who has recently graduated from college and has returned home, not as prepared to take on the world as anticipated. This stranger may be another mother who needs help but who is hesitant to ask. Or perhaps the stranger is one of our children's friends, whose home life is not everything it could be. Mothers, let us keep our eyes open to the opportunities God may put before us and be hospitable to someone in need, as Laurie was in her story above. Hebrews 13:1-2 says, "Continue to love each other like brothers (sisters), and remember always to welcome strangers, for by doing this, some people have entertained angels without knowing it." Once we open our eyes, the need we see can be overwhelming. We cannot let that stop us, not just for the needs of the people we see around us, but because we need to model it for our children. So let us follow Saint Teresa of Calcutta's advice, "Don't worry about the numbers. Help one person at a time and always start with the person nearest you."

***

Homework from Heaven

"Hospitality"

What to Do:
1. Invite someone from your church who may live alone or who doesn't have family living nearby to join your family for Sunday dinner.
2. Help local shelters with needed supplies to make their "strangers" feel more welcome and comfortable.

***
Prayerful Pause

*Dear Jesus,
Please help us to be more aware
of the people around us who may need our
hospitality.
Amen.*

***
Memos to Me

***
Pondering through Pictures

Clothe the Naked

***

Mary's Memory

"The Magic of Duct Tape & Super Glue™"

My son, Patrick "clothed the naked" his senior year in high school. He spent a semester volunteering in a first-grade classroom. The school was in an area where children lived in poverty. One day, it was wet outside, but not so wet to stop outdoor recess. As the children shuffled out, Patrick noticed one boy who was not going outside. He turned to the teacher, and she indicated for him to see what was the matter. Patrick asked the boy, "What's up?" The boy turned a little red in the face and showed Patrick the bottom of his shoe. It had a big hole in it, and Patrick saw his sock. Patrick understood and asked the boy if he would give him the shoe. The boy did. Then, Patrick asked the teacher if he could go to his car for a few minutes while showing her the bottom of the shoe. She allowed it. Patrick had duct tape and Super Glue™ in his car, and he wrapped and wrapped and wrapped around that shoe and sealed it with Super Glue™. Then, he brought the shoe back to the classroom and asked the teacher if he could borrow her colored Sharpies™. She gave them to him, and Patrick brought them and the shoe to the little boy.

They spent the rest of recess making that shoe the coolest! When the other children came back, they all wanted one too. Later at conferences, the grandmother came in and told the teacher that she was going to buy her grandson new shoes, but he wasn't havin' it - he thought he had the best shoe right there on his foot.

***
Heavenly Hint

"Whoever is kind to the poor is lending to Yahweh Who will repay him the kindness done."
Proverbs 19:17

***
Reflection

    Jesus' fourth invitation to love and serve is to "Clothe the Naked." What does the Bible tell us about clothing a person? In Colossians 3:12,14, it states, "As the chosen of God, then, the holy people whom He loves, you are to be clothed in heartfelt compassion, in generosity and humility, gentleness and patience. Over all these clothes, put on love, the perfect bond." Patrick, who could have been intimidating to this small boy because he is six feet five inches, instead was a gentle giant and showed each of these virtues in the above story. Not only did he bind a child's shoe with duct tape and Super Glue™, but he also did so with love, which made it perfect in the child's eyes.

    Moms, we should make it a practice to clothe our children with heartfelt mercy. Cover their tears with kindness and patience, and above all, love them with everything we have. For as Saint Teresa of Calcutta says, "Love begins at home, and it is not how much we do, but how much love we put in that action."

***
Homework from Heaven

"Lend to the Lord"

What to Do:

In our reflection, we did not address the traditional meaning of "clothe the naked." So, we are emphasizing it here. Below are a few places we suggest giving clothes to people who may need them.

1. Bring women's clothes and toiletries, baby clothes and diapers, as well as toys to a women's shelter or a Crisis Pregnancy Center. Keep in mind premature sizes too.
2. Instead of having a garage sale, donate the clothes to a local charity such as Saint Vincent de Paul or Goodwill.
3. Giving hand-me-downs to family, friends, or neighbors. Share the wealth, especially the younger clothes that children grow out of so quickly.

***

Prayerful Pause

Dearest Jesus,
Please help us to be attentive
to those around us so that when we see a
soul in need, we take the time to clothe
them in Your love.
Amen.

***
Memos to Me

_____

_____

_____

_____

_____

_____

_____

***
Pondering through Pictures

Visit the Sick & Imprisoned

***

Mary's Memory
"We're Going to the Circus"

I visited the sick and imprisoned when I was a senior in high school. I had committed to volunteer in a nursing home Monday through Friday, for an hour each day. The activity director asked me to work with a gentleman named Jim because his family never came to visit him, and he sat in his room alone most of the time. Jim did not know how long he had been there, and no one had ever taken him for an outing. The director hoped I could draw Jim out of his room and help him participate in the center's activities.

Throughout the year, Jim and I became very close. We both looked forward to our time together. Then, one day around January, Jim told me that he had advanced cancer in his leg and that the only means of getting it was to cut off his leg from the knee down. Then, he told me he would let himself die because Jim thought he was a burden on his family. I fought hard, lovingly, but hard against Jim. I reminded him of how much I loved him and how it would affect me. Eventually, Jim agreed. He had the surgery, and it appeared that he had beaten it too, until May, when the doctor once again found cancer and could not find a path to health. Jim was dying. We continued our daily visits until the end.

At one of those visits, I told Jim about a traveling circus one of my teachers used to be in and that it was coming to town. Jim smiled and said he had never been to a circus but had always wanted to go. My wheels started spinning. I went to my teacher, explained the situation, and asked if he would help me get Jim to the circus. My teacher agreed and talked to his colleagues, the circus performers. They set it up so that Jim was a VIP at the performance. When I brought the idea to the activity director, she told me not to get my hopes up because she'd have to get the family's permission, and they seldom responded. However, the family did respond. They wanted to know who I was to Jim. The activity director explained that I was a volunteer who had become friends with Jim throughout the year. The family agreed to the circus adventure. So, Jim and I enjoyed the circus one warm evening in May and even got to go behind the scenes with my teacher to meet the performers. It was wonderful! Even more remarkable was that Jim's family started to visit him again. They spent the last month of his life with him, as Jim died that June. I still treasure my photograph of Jim with his big smile.

***

Heavenly Hint

"'And when was it that we saw You sick or in prison and visited You?' And the King will answer them, 'Truly I tell you, just as you did it to one of the least of these who are members of My family, you did it to Me.'"
Matthew 25:39-40

***

Reflection

Jesus' fifth and sixth invitations to love and serve are to "Visit the Sick" and to "Visit the Imprisoned." Saint Catherine Laboure once said, "See the face of God in everyone." Mary did that every time she visited her friend Jim. She also allowed Jim's family to see the face of God in their father before he died.

Our children can sometimes feel like Jim. Jim's family ignored him and kept telling him they did not have time to visit him, and he was lonely because of it. Moms, our children yearn for our attention. If our days get too busy for them, then we risk leaving our children, like Jim, feeling ignored, lonely, and perhaps even "imprisoned," especially the little ones. Laurie discovered she was guilty of this during a very hectic time because one of Laurie's kids said to her, "Mom, you're always doing things for us, but you never do anything with us." That was very eye-opening for Laurie. When Laurie told Mary this, she answered, "That's true. We have to be careful not to busy our children out of our lives - they need us." Moms, we need to be mindful to take the time to be present to our children both in their daily needs and in their spontaneous needs.

Now, let us turn our attention to Jesus' invitation to visit the sick. As we all know, with children comes illness. Someone who is sick is vulnerable. So, we need to take care of not only their physical body but their mind and heart as well. We should be open to dropping some things off the to-do list and instead spending time with our child. We recommend mothers heed Saint Benedict of Nursia, "Before all, and above all, attention shall be paid to the care of the sick so that they shall be served as if they were Christ Himself." Mary did this by making a "nest" on the couch and having her children come lay down in the nest, bringing with them the special things that comforted them. Then, she would cozy them in and put on their favorite show or play soothing music. The kids usually fell in and out of sleep, but ultimately it was Mary's way of tending to their needs. She made sure she was present and available to cuddle or play games with them when they were awake. So, when our children are sick, moms, may we be there for them as if they were Christ Himself.

***
Homework from Heaven
"Doing Things Together"

What to Do:
1. Make sure you give time to your children every day. Not doing things just for them, but also with them.
2. Visit someone who could be considered "imprisoned" in their own home and bring your child with you. Mary did this when Maggie was four. One of Mary's friends asked her to visit her mom whose memory was failing, and who was alone all day. Mary agreed and on her first visit, found out in a conversation with her, she loved the movie, "Mary Poppins." Coincidentally, so did Maggie. So, when they came, Mary would fix or bring lunch for her. This woman loved having Maggie there. After lunch, she would play games like I-Spy with Maggie or read a children's book or two that Mary would bring with her. Finally, to her friend's mom's delight, Mary would pull out of her bag the movie, "Mary Poppins." This kind woman would not remember that they had watched it the week before and every time she would say, "I loved this movie when I was young!" So, they would all settle in and watch the movie together before Mary and Maggie had to leave.
3. Consider making homemade cards and/or flowers. The flowers can be handmade, silk, or fresh. Share these, along with your loving heart, with the older men and women living in nursing homes or are homebound. Your church may be able to provide you with names and addresses.

*** Prayerful Pause

Oh Lord,
May we continue to love one another as brothers and sisters, regardless of our circumstances.
Amen.

***
Memos to Me

_____

_____

_____

_____

_____

_____

_____

***
Pondering through Pictures

Lay to Rest

***

Mary's Memory

"Innocent Eyes"

I was eight months pregnant at my mom's funeral. My son, Patrick was six years old, and my daughter Kathleen was four. The two of them charmed my mother's loved ones with their innocent eyes. Even Maggie, who was not yet born, brought joy to the funeral. I doubt if there was one person there who did not touch my pregnant belly. The funeral was lovely. I felt as if my dad had escorted his beloved wife home, as her funeral was on the day Dad died, what I like to affectionately call my dad's Feast Day.

***

Heavenly Hint

"The dust returns to the earth from which it came, and the spirit returns to God Who gave it."
Ecclesiastes 12:7

***

Reflection

The seventh and final invitation to love and serve is to "Bury the Dead." It is important to teach our children to honor our loved ones when they die. We do this by taking them to funerals. While it is sad, our children learn to honor people and the importance of blessing and putting the bodies of those who have died to rest. Scripture tells us in Psalm 116:15, "Precious in the sight of the Lord is the death of his faithful ones."

Bringing our children to funerals also teaches them that the funeral is as much for those of us left behind as it is for the deceased. They see us saying goodbye and sharing stories of this person who we all loved. They see how we comfort each other, how we accept comfort ourselves, and how we can be a comfort to someone else. An anonymous author expressed it beautifully, "A child at a funeral is like a bird before dawn because they don't need the sun to come up before they start singing the new day's song. They bring us hope in our hour of darkness." All three happened at the funeral of Mary's mom. Ultimately, Mary's children were taught about sympathy and empathy while honoring their grandma, or Munna, as they still call her today.

***

Homework from Heaven

"Rosaries, Flowers & Flags"

What to Do:
1. Have a rosary service before the Funeral Mass of a loved one.
2. Bring flowers to a loved one's gravesite or bring flags to the graves of soldiers on Memorial Day.

✱✱✱
Prayerful Pause

*Jesus,
May we remember and respect
the importance of blessing and putting the
body of those we love to rest.
Amen.*

***
Memos to Me

_____
_____
_____
_____
_____
_____
_____

***
Pondering through Pictures

The Spirit of Jesus

***

"You know well enough that our Lord does not look so much at the greatness of our actions, nor even at their difficulty, but at the love with which we do them."
Saint Thérèse of Lisieux

Living Jesus' Verbs

***

Mercy is a crucial message in the Gospels. We have already discussed the Corporal Works of Mercy, where scripture calls us to be the Body of Christ to each other by caring for one another's physical needs. Caring for one another's physical needs is an integral part of being a Christian. Yet, God calls us to imitate the mercy of our Lord by taking care of each other's spiritual needs as well. The Spiritual Works of Mercy meet this call.

We never know when a moment will come that God will call us to use the Spiritual Works of Mercy. However, when we find ourselves in a situation where He does, we should not hesitate. By not hesitating, we mean to either act right then or if unsure how to act, take the time to pray and discern how to best use His work of mercy to help the situation. Never forget the inspiring and challenging words of Jesus in Matthew 25:40, "Truly I tell you, just as you did it to one of the least of these who are members of my family, you did it to Me."

Spiritual Works

***

Instruct the ignorant

Counsel the doubtful

Admonish the sinner

Bear wrongs patiently

Forgive offenses willingly

Comfort the afflicted

Pray for the living and the dead

Teaching with Kindness

***

Laurie's Story

"What Bunk Beds Were Really Made For"

It was a rainy Washington afternoon, and Mary and her girls had come down for a visit. My daughter, Amy, had just celebrated her eleventh birthday when she got two kittens, who she named Phillip and Aurora. Amy was not at home, and the rest of the girls were being creative with their time. There were five of them between the ages of nine and four and two kittens. So, when we say creative, we mean creative. Unbeknownst to us, in the kitchen, the girls took a large folding plastic table and opened two legs. Next, they slid the legs under the top mattress of the girl's low bunk bed, creating a slide out of the table. After the kids put pillows and blankets all around the table, they started sliding down on top of the spare blankets to go faster. The girls soon squealed with delight as they took turns going down the "slide."

Then, one of the girls got the crazy idea that the kittens would enjoy sliding too. It was about that time when Mary's oldest daughter, Kathleen, who was a year older than my daughter, Rose, walked in with Sarah, who was a little less than a year old. When she saw Phillip sailing down the table, she said, "Don't put the kittens on the slide; it could hurt them." Mind you, she did not give the danger of the slide, in general, a second thought. Just then, Aurora hit the ground with a thud after whipping down the table. Kathleen set Sarah down and ran for the kittens. Kathleen scooped Phillip and Aurora up and gave them some "sugar." Instead of going and telling on the younger girls, Kathleen calmed the kittens down, while gently explaining to them that the kittens were just babies and could get hurt. Then, Kathleen put them out of the room because she figured it was her turn to go down the slide.

***
Heavenly Hint

*"Let the Word of Christ,
in all its richness, find a home with you.
Teach each other, and advise each other,
in all wisdom."*
Colossians 3:16

***
Reflection

The first Spiritual Work of Mercy is to instruct the ignorant; ignorant meaning lacking knowledge, information, or awareness about something. Laurie's story above is an excellent example of this. The kittens were the Robbins' first pets, and the children did not know that putting the kittens down the slide could hurt them. Kathleen already knew this because she grew up with little dogs and was taught what could hurt them. The younger girls were in a state of ignorance. They were unaware of the danger to the kittens as they went down such a steep slide, so Kathleen took the time to kindly teach them. That is what instructing the ignorant means, teaching someone something they do not already know about or are unaware of. We need to be like Kathleen, ready to teach with kindness, but on a much greater scope.

Moms, we said in the Opening of the book it is our "soul" purpose to teach our children about the Blessed Trinity so that they will someday live with Him in heaven. Our children come to us ignorant of the faith. In Deuteronomy 6:7, God calls us to instruct our children about Him. He makes it clear that He wants it forefront in our minds as we go about our days together: "Let the words I (God) enjoin on you today stay in your heart. You shall tell them to your children, and keep on telling them, when you are sitting at home, when you are out and about, when you are lying down and when you are standing up…" God is saying that we are to seek opportunities and take the time to instruct our children about Him.

However, instruction is not only given by word of mouth. We teach through our actions and in our attitude. As Saint Francis of Assisi said, "Preach the gospel at all times, and if necessary, use words." Our faith should bring us joy. If we as moms walk around as grump-a-lumps and complain about all our tasks, how are we bringing our children joy? As Saint Teresa of Calcutta taught us, "God likes a cheerful worker." We are teaching our children about how to behave each day through our actions. If we model being grumpy about doing tasks, our children will likely be grumpy about their tasks. When young, our children are like sponges. They soak up the things that they see and hear then copy them. Let them see us be cheerful workers.

Modeling our faith is necessary, as we have discussed throughout this book, but our attitude about our faith counts too. Having a relationship with God should be something we want and learning about Him should be a joy. Since our children soak up their world like sponges, let us take advantage of it by making learning about God a joy. This way, as they learn about God, they will hopefully keep wanting more.

Our purpose is to teach our children about God, and that purpose does not end when they leave our house. We continue to show them the joys of faith until we are no longer with them. So let us hold our heads high and accept the authority God has given us and let His light shine through us. Let it come out of our mouths, model it, and share it with our children joyfully. Keep at it tenaciously so that as they grow, the memories and stories of how we learned about faith as a family will be told over and over again.

***
Homework from Heaven
"We're in This Together"

What to Do:
1. Join a mom's group or contact friends who are moms and regularly get together with them. You can mutually support each other so that you don't have to feel as if you're alone throughout your vocation of motherhood.
2. Join in with the activities of your parish. For example, sign your younger children up for Vacation Bible School in the summer and encourage your older children to volunteer. If you can, join in the fun.
3. For the older ones, find retreats and a youth group, hopefully in your own parish.
4. Encourage your children to volunteer in the parish community. For example, they could help out at coffee and donuts, clean the church, or help take care of the grounds. Even the little ones can help pull weeds.
5. Have your children participate at church, like Mary's son Patrick who ushered with his dad, altar serving like Laurie's sons Sam and Jonathan, or singing in the choir like Laurie's girls.

***
Prayerful Pause

*Dear Jesus,
Let us breathe our faith
like we breathe the air. Help us to speak it,
live it, and share it with joy so that our
children in kind will know it, live it, and
love it all the days of their lives.
Amen.*

***
Memos to Me

_____
_____
_____
_____
_____
_____
_____

***
Pondering through Pictures

Eyes on the Prize

***

Mary's Memory

"Letting Go"

Laurie and I put together an overnight retreat for moms. At the retreat, we provided the opportunity to go to the Sacrament of Reconciliation. One mother turned to me and said she was afraid to go and was never really sure if it was necessary. I told her that going to reconciliation is a beautiful way to let go of things we've done wrong or things we have hung onto that hurt us. I reassured the mom by telling her that there was no need to be afraid. "The priest is there for you and will help you draw closer to God." The mom smiled and told me that she did not remember what to do during reconciliation or the prayer she was supposed to say. I told the mom that Father was here for her and that knowing the exact words didn't matter. "Just be yourself, and Father Sean will guide you." The mom went to reconciliation. When she came out, she told me she was glad to have gone and thanked me.

***

Heavenly Hint

"When there are some who have doubts reassure them..."
Jude 1:22

***
Reflection

The second Spiritual Work of Mercy is to counsel the doubtful. Throughout our lives, we all will experience doubts in our faith life. We can count on Jesus to be there to silence our doubts. Jesus came that we may have a life with joy and not with worry or doubt. We need to keep our eyes on the prize, as the expression goes. When we doubt, we take our eyes off Jesus and His promises to us. Peter took his eyes off of Jesus in Matthew 14: 23-31:

> "When evening came, He was there alone, while the boat, by now some furlongs from land, was hard pressed by rough waves, for there was a head wind. In the fourth watch of the night, He came towards them, walking on the sea, and when the disciples saw Him walking on the sea, they were terrified. 'It is a ghost,' they said, and cried out in fear. But at once Jesus called out to them, saying, 'Courage! It's me! Don't be afraid.' It was Peter who answered. 'Lord,' he said, 'if it is You, tell me to come to You across the water.' Jesus said, 'Come.' Then Peter got out of the boat and started walking towards Jesus across the water, but then noticing the wind, he took fright and began to sink. 'Lord,' he cried, 'save me!' Jesus put out His hand at once and held him."

When Peter took his eyes off of Jesus, doubts set in, and he fell in the water. As he began sinking, Peter called out to Jesus for help. Jesus did not hesitate - at once He stretched out His hand and held Peter. He loved Peter deeply and immediately protected Him and calmed his fear and doubt. Jesus is always ready to do the same for us. When doubt or fear troubles our mind, unlike Peter in that moment, let us remember to keep our eyes on the prize. Jesus is that prize!

When our children doubt, which they will, they need to know that all they have to do is call out or pray to Jesus. He will be there for them whether they feel it or not. We need to be there for them too. As Saint John Bosco once said, "It is not enough to love the children, it is necessary that they are aware that they are loved." We love our children by confidently letting them know of God's love for them whether they are doubting or not. They must know that they can come to us and express their doubt to us. They can ask their questions safely and not feel judged. Our children need to know that it is okay to doubt. Neither God nor we will think less of them. We all have doubts on occasion, much like the mom in Mary's Memory.

In her memory above, Mary gently quelled the doubts of the mother by counseling her through her fear and doubt. Mary did not rush her. Instead, she gave the woman both her presence and time, which allowed the woman to get to the underlying reason that was holding her back.

As moms, we need to give our children the same respect, presence, and time that Mary gave to the woman at the retreat. Our children need both our presence and time when they are in doubt. Help them to determine the root of their doubt by asking questions and listening to their answers. Give them time to think without being impatient. Let them know we are there with them and for them throughout the conversation. Accept their thoughts without judgment, while at the same time engaging them. Reassure them that it is okay to have doubts, but not to stay stuck there. If we are not sure how to answer their questions, be honest, and research together to find information to address the doubt. In this way, we know the information gathered comes from reliable sources because we were actively involved in the research and took the time to help our child find those answers.

When we welcome our children's questions and find answers with them patiently and lovingly, we are showing them how important faith is and how much we love sharing it with them. Surely, in doing this, we are helping them to accept the outstretched hand that Jesus continually offers them. That is what the second Spiritual Work of Mercy is all about - helping someone unsure about their faith and encouraging them along their journey.

***

Homework from Heaven
"Addressing Doubts"

What to Do:
1. Sit down with your children and together find Bible verses that encourage your children to have faith in God, and when in doubt, turn to Him. Write these scriptures down on index cards so that when your child is doubtful, they can read these verses and strengthen their faith. Perhaps put them near their bed, so they always know where to find them.
2. Take them to Grandma, Grandpa, or someone both you and your child respect. Talk to the person about your child's particular doubt. Let them witness the strong faith of the person that they care about as they address the doubt. After the person has finished speaking, if your child does not ask a question, you ask one so as to start a conversation, then let it flow naturally. This person's living example of faith will hopefully strengthen your child's.
3. Turn to the saints and see how they dealt with doubts. Help your child find a saint who struggled with a similar doubt, or your child's specific doubt and how they dealt with it.
4. Two more important ways to quiet a child's doubt are to say prayers with them asking for Jesus' help and to sing songs with them that will bolster their faith and speak to their soul.

***
Prayerful Pause

*Dearest Jesus,
May we give both our children
and others our presence and time to
reassure them when they are doubting.
Help them to feel loved and accepted as
we together seek Your Truth.
Amen.*

*** *Memos to Me*

*** *Pondering through Pictures*

Take Pause

***

Mary's Memory

"God's Smile"

One evening, I was giving my four-year-old son, Patrick, a bath. He was having fun squirting what he called "grunch" all over himself. Grunch to you and me is bath foam soap. He kept dropping the bottle in the water, which ruined the foam because water got into the canister. I asked Patrick repeatedly not to leave the grunch in the water. Frustrated, I finally said, "Patrick, I do not want to see the grunch in the water again, or I will take it away for the rest of your bath." He dropped it in the water once again. I asked, "Did I just see you drop the grunch in the water again?" Patrick denied dropping the canister into the water and said, "Mama, I didn't do it!" Rather than getting angry with Patrick for lying to me, I decided to give him a second chance. I told him how important it is to tell the truth and how God smiles on people who do. Then, I said, "I'm going to ask you a question. Who dropped the grunch in the water?" Patrick whispered back, "Patrick." I squealed with delight, cheering that Patrick had told me the truth. Patrick beamed and said, "I just made God smile!" I answered, "That's right, Patrick, and I am so proud of you."

***
Heavenly Hint

*"Brothers (and sisters),
even if one of you is caught doing
something wrong, those of you who are
spiritual should set that person right in a
spirit of gentleness; and watch yourselves
that you are not put to the
test in the same way."
Galatians 6:1*

***
Reflection

The third work of mercy is to admonish the sinner. This work of mercy is a difficult one. To admonish is to counsel against something mildly and courteously. We are not meant to be judges, for God alone holds that position. However, we cannot allow our children to remain in sin without correction. Our job is to teach them how to stop and do what is right when temptation strikes. That is incredibly tough if a group of peers is pressuring them, but let us teach them what Saint Augustine said, "Right is right even if no one is doing it; wrong is wrong even if everyone is doing it." When someone is tempted, Jesus has taught us to help that person by teaching or encouraging them to do what is right.

Mary showed mercy on Patrick in the above story. She could have gotten angry and punished Patrick for lying. Instead, in a mild-mannered way, she used the situation as a teachable moment, explained the importance of telling the truth, and gave Patrick a second chance. With one merciful choice, a story that could have ended in anger, ended with Patrick being proud of himself for telling the truth.

What Mary did with Patrick at four years old is a good example of how to admonish our younger children, but this approach will not work with our older ones. As our children age, peers carry a big influence on them. Too often, people think it is funny to tease and play dirty tricks on others. Laughing with them condones the behavior. Mary's friend once told her that while with a group of friends, someone shared a story about a dirty trick he had played on someone in high school. It was a hurtful trick. Everyone began laughing. Mary's friend did not find it funny. So, she asked, "I wonder how the person who was tricked felt?" That was a gentle way to admonish someone because it stopped the laughter and made everyone think. When done gently, that is what admonishing the sinner can do - help people take pause.

Another way to help our older children is to teach them not to contribute to things like gossip. By not taking place in things such as gossip, we are indirectly admonishing the sinner. Saint John Vianney suggests three ways of dealing with gossip, "If something uncharitable is said in your presence, either speak in favor of the absent, or withdraw, or if possible, stop the conversation." When we encourage each other not to sin by not contributing to it, we help each other to live as Jesus taught us.

***

Homework from Heaven

"Second Chances"

What to Do:
1. Stay open to giving your child a second chance to make the right choice, as Mary did in the above story. Some wrong choices can be teachable moments or are lessons learned in and of themselves. A lot can be learned when giving our children grace. Hopefully, they, in turn, learn to give grace to others.
2. Our children will have a better chance at learning to give

grace if it is not only given to them, but they watch us give it to others as well. Second chances are not just for children. We all make poor choices at times, and we all need grace because of it, no matter our age.

***

Prayerful Pause

*Dear Jesus,
Please help us to be mild and courteous when admonishing our children, and may we also choose to avoid participating in sin, thus encouraging others
to do the same.
Amen.*

***
Memos to Me

_____
_____
_____
_____
_____
_____
_____

***
Pondering through Pictures

Set Pride Aside

***

Mary's Memory

"Pursue Peace"

Maggie and her friends were winding down lunch when one friend turned to the other and asked if she would go to the nurse's office with her to give the nurse a letter. Maggie grabbed her friend's milk and jokingly said, "I won't give it back unless you stay with me." The girl who needed to go to the nurse looked at Maggie and said, "She should be able to make her own decisions." "I was just kidding," Maggie responded. Maggie's friend took the milk back and got up, saying, "I'm not going." then walked away. The girl needing to go to the nurse looked at Maggie and said, "You're mean." Maggie gave her a puzzled look. Then, the girl turned on Maggie, saying, "You're a witch!" but not nicely, because it was spelled with a b, not a w. Without malice, Maggie returned with, "I don't care what you think of me." and walked away, both confused and hurt.

Once she got home, Maggie told Mary about the incident. Mary asked her if she had ever done anything to the girl in the past. Maggie hadn't. Then, Mary asked if Maggie had told anyone else about what had happened. Maggie hadn't. Mary asked one final question, "Do you think anyone's feelings were hurt besides yours?" Thinking about it for a moment, Maggie realized that maybe she had unintentionally hurt her friend's feelings. The following Monday, Maggie went to the girl who had called her a name and apologized for what had happened, explaining that she was just playing and meant nothing by it. The girl told Maggie that it was not her fault and that she was in a bad mood that day. Then, the girl apologized to Maggie, and it was over. Maggie's pursuit of peace worked, and the girls are still great friends to this day.

***

Heavenly Hint

"So then, let us be always seeking the ways which lead to peace and the ways in which we can support one another."
Romans 14:19

***

Reflection

The fourth and fifth Spiritual Works of Mercy are to bear wrongs patiently and to forgive offenses willingly. Bearing wrongs patiently and forgiving offenses willingly are not always easy. Sometimes, our pride can get in the way. In the gospel of Luke 6:27-28,31, Jesus guides us by saying, "But I say this to you who are listening: Love your enemies, do good to those who hate you, bless those who curse you, pray for those who treat you badly. Treat others as you would like people to treat you." It is not always easy to follow this call. However, Jesus will guide us and give us people to help us along the way.

Bearing wrongs patiently and forgiving offenses willingly can be a struggle for youth. Mary's daughter, Maggie, experienced this. It is not enough to bear wrongs patiently and forgive offenses willingly without examining our behavior as well. We ought to heed the scripture in Matthew 7:3 which asks us, "Why do you observe the splinter in your brother's (sister's) eye and never notice the great log in your own?" Keep in mind that while we may be bearing someone else's wrongs patiently, they may also be bearing ours.

In the memory above, Mary had Maggie reflect on her behavior, which led to a peaceful resolution. As the adage says, "It takes two to tango." As Maggie reflected on her behavior, she realized that she may have been unintentionally hurtful. She set her pride aside and was willing to ask her friend to forgive her. By doing this, Maggie's friend considered her part in the confrontation. It allowed her friend to set her pride aside as well. She then chose to ask forgiveness of Maggie in turn. Forgiveness built up their friendship and fostered peace between them, thus fully restoring their friendship, a friendship they hold dear to this day.

Mothers, it is essential to teach our children to bear with others patiently, forgive wrongs willingly, and strive to live in such a way that as Saint Bridget of Sweden once said, "We must show love for those who do evil to us and pray for them. Nothing is more dearer or more pleasing to God than this."

***

Homework from Heaven

"Answer the Call"

What to Do:

1. Encourage your children to answer Jesus' call by treating people the way they would want to be treated. Remind them to think about their behavior before they act. Suggest they ask themselves the question, "How would I feel if I were treated that way?" Have them imagine themselves being in the other person's shoes and depending on how it felt, let that lead to how they choose to behave. This way, perhaps it can stop them from doing something hurtful, and they can avoid having others bear their wrongs or needing to ask for forgiveness at all.
2. When someone hurts your children, help them to reflect on their behavior to determine if they may have hurt that person also. If they have, teach them to pray, asking God for the grace to set aside any pride and ask for forgiveness.

***
Prayerful Pause

*Dear Jesus,
May we always strive to treat others the way we would like to be treated. If we do hurt someone, help us to seek peaceful resolutions and ask for forgiveness.
Amen.*

***
Memos to Me

_____

_____

_____

_____

_____

_____

_____

***
Pondering through Pictures

At the Center is Love & Grace

***

Laurie's Story

"Teamwork"

It was a Saturday morning when Mary and her girls came to visit. Once they arrived, everyone dispersed throughout the house for fun and laughter. Everything was going along fine when my fifth child Rebekah came to me in distress. She was having an anxiety attack but was too upset to take her daily anxiety medication. She told me her stomach was upset as well. Rebekah was pacing from room to room and would sit down and then get back up and return to pacing. Rebekah finally told me that she wanted her sister Amy. I gave Amy a call, as she had left earlier in the day to celebrate a friend's birthday. Amy had had a lot of experience with her own anxiety and returned home as quickly as she could.

When Amy arrived, she hugged Rebekah and led her to the couch. Rebekah put her head in Amy's lap, and I sat beside Amy and began gently rubbing Rebekah's head. Mary rounded the corner and sat at Rebekah's feet. She noticed that Rebekah was cold. So, she got a blanket and wrapped Rebekah up tight and then turned on the T.V. and asked Rebekah what she wanted to watch. Mary's intention was to take Rebekah's mind off her anxiety. Before we knew it, Rebekah was able to calm down enough to take her medicine.

***

Heavenly Hint

"As one whom his mother comforts, so I will comfort you..."
Isaiah 66:13

***

Reflection

We have all experienced that moment when someone else is hurting, and all we can do is be there with them. We know that this is not enough, yet it may be all we are able to offer. This situation exemplifies the sixth Spiritual Work of Mercy to comfort the afflicted. Comforting the afflicted is to help others cope with difficulties. In Luke 24:13-32, Jesus did this for two of His disciples who were walking in sorrow three days after His crucifixion:

> "That very day two of them were going to a village named Emmaus, about seven miles from Jerusalem, and talking with each other about all these things that had happened. While they were talking and discussing together, Jesus Himself drew near and went with them. But their eyes were kept from recognizing Him. And He said to them, "What is this conversation which you are holding with each other as you walk?" And they stood still, looking sad. Then one of them, named Cle′opas, answered Him, "Are you the only visitor to Jerusalem who does not know the things that have happened there in these days?" And He said to them, "What things?" And they said to Him, "Concerning Jesus of Nazareth, who was a prophet mighty in deed and

word before God and all the people, and how our chief priests and rulers delivered him up to be condemned to death and crucified Him. But we had hoped that He was the one to redeem Israel. Yes, and besides all this, it is now the third day since this happened. Moreover, some women of our company amazed us. They were at the tomb early in the morning and did not find His body; and they came back saying that they had even seen a vision of angels, who said that He was alive. Some of those who were with us went to the tomb and found it just as the women had said; but Him they did not see." And He said to them, "O foolish men, and slow of heart to believe all that the prophets have spoken! Was it not necessary that the Christ should suffer these things and enter into His glory?" And beginning with Moses and all the prophets, He interpreted to them in all the scriptures the things concerning Himself.

So, they drew near to the village to which they were going. He appeared to be going further, but they constrained Him, saying, "Stay with us, for it is toward evening and the day is now far spent." So, He went in to stay with them. When He was at table with them, He took the bread and blessed, and broke it, and gave it to them. And their eyes were opened, and they recognized Him; and He vanished out of their sight. They said to each other, "Did not our hearts burn within us while He talked to us on the road, while He opened to us the scriptures?"

There are times when the people in our lives are afflicted, and we feel as if there is nothing we can do to help. In the scripture above, the disciples' affliction was a deep sorrow. Jesus' response was to enter into their suffering. He walked with them and let them talk to Him and tell Him why they were so sad. Then, He spoke to them, and His words helped them. Jesus chose to be there and share in the heartache. In doing so, lifted them up.

What Jesus did for the disciples, He calls us to do for each other. Jesus did not tell them to come to Him, to go to the temple, or to ask for help. No, Jesus came to His disciples and accepted them where they were at, right in the midst of their sorrow, and took the time to comfort them. Jesus demonstrated to us what Saint Francis de Sales told us, "Never miss an opportunity to do good." When we see someone suffering, Jesus calls us to help. He calls us to bring His goodness and love to the afflicted, thereby allaying their suffering.

In Laurie's Story, Rebekah was temporarily afflicted with anxiety. Together, Laurie, Amy, and Mary dropped everything and came to Rebekah. They took care of Rebekah and allowed God's love to lift her up through their love for her. These two examples of affliction ended quickly, but not all will. Sometimes when we choose to enter into someone else's suffering, it will not be quick. Long-suffering will require our presence, time, love, and patience, to help someone through their pain. Our love and support bring consistent comfort to that person. We help them to feel loved when they need it most. This is what comforting the afflicted looks like. Sometimes it falls on us alone, while other times it takes a team. Inevitably, it always takes a willingness to share in the suffering with that person so that the love and grace of our Lord Jesus can be in the center of it to comfort them through it.

***

Homework from Heaven

"Allaying Affliction"

What to Do:
1. If we find our family or friends somehow afflicted, we can listen to them, offer to read scripture or pray with them.
2. Here are a few questions you can reflect on regarding your children's afflictions:

a. What brings fear into my children's hearts? How are they comforted?
b. Do I take my children's concerns seriously and attend to their worries?
c. Do I offer my support and reassurance?
d. Do I pray with/for my children to help calm them?

***

Prayerful Pause

Sweet Jesus,
Help me to recognize Your call to share in someone's suffering or sorrow, especially when it's my children. Use me to help lift others up and allay their suffering when they need it most.
Amen.

***
Memos to Me

_____

_____

_____

_____

_____

_____

_____

***
Pondering through Pictures

Pray for God's People

***

Laurie's Story

"Rest in Peace"

When Steve and I got married, he shared with me a family tradition that he grew up with. After saying Grace, the prayer before meals, Steve's family added on, "May all the souls of the faithful departed, through the mercy of God, rest in peace. Amen." Given that we pray this before each meal of the day, we end up praying many prayers for those who have gone before us.

As Mary and I hung out over the years, we would say Grace together, and she liked the additional prayer so much that her family added it too. I'm very thankful that Steve shared this with me and that our family carries on his family's tradition.

***

Heavenly Hint

"Never get tired of staying awake to pray for all God's holy people..."
Ephesians 6:18

***

Reflection

The seventh and final Spiritual Work of Mercy is to pray for the living and the dead. Mary tells her children that while she cannot serve like she used to due to arthritis, she can be a prayer warrior.

Teaching our children to pray for others is part of an active Christian lifestyle. The first part of this Spiritual Work of Mercy tells us to pray for the living. There are many scripture verses that demonstrate praying for the living. In John 17:11, Jesus prayed, "I am no longer in the world, but they are in the world, and I am coming to You. Holy Father, keep those You have given Me true to Your name, so that they may be one like Us." And in John 17:15-17, He prayed, "I am not asking You to remove them from the world, but to protect them from the evil one. They do not belong to the world any more than I belong to the world. Consecrate them in truth; Your word is truth." These are only two of many verses that Jesus demonstrates praying for the living.

We build each other up through prayer. We ease each other's suffering through prayer. Praying for one another brings comfort and hope. While it is important to pray for those we know and love, it is also important to pray for those who have no one to pray for them. Jesus hears all of our prayers and honors the hearts of those who care about all of His brothers and sisters. Our prayers provide comfort and hope even when the person is unaware that we are praying for them. Jesus is that good. Jesus loves us that much. It is imperative that we teach our children to model Jesus' example and pray for others.

The second part of this spiritual gift is to pray for the dead. Scripture encourages us to pray in Philippians 4:6, "Never worry about anything; but tell God all your desires of every kind in prayer and petition shot through with gratitude..." This Scripture tells us to bring any concern of ours in thanksgiving and God will bring us peace. When someone we love dies, we need not worry. We can pray for God's mercy that they will be safely delivered to Him in heaven, just like Laurie's and Mary's families do before each meal.

Moms, it is essential that we teach our children the Spiritual Works of Mercy. Let us listen to the words Jesus told Saint Faustina. "He (Jesus) desires that we practice at least one act of mercy every day. He specified that mercy could be carried out in one of three manners: by kind words, by kind deeds, and by prayer." Throughout this book, we have already discussed the importance of doing kind deeds and saying kind words, but we cannot emphasize enough the significance and power of prayer. Let us never forget to pray for one another as well as those who have gone before us.

***

Homework from Heaven

"Votive Candles"/ "Mercy Cards"/ "Don't Hesitate"

Materials: "Votive Candles"
- Small glass votive candle holders including candles
- Small letter and decorative stickers

What to Do: For Younger Children
1. Gather the family and choose the name of a family member or friend who has passed away.
2. Using the small letter stickers, spell out the name of that person on the votive candle holder.
3. Add cross and flower stickers as desired and put in candle.
4. Light the candle and set it by the picture of the loved one.
5. Let this candle remind the family to pray for them.
6. Light the candle on November 2nd, which is All Souls' Day, on the anniversary of their death, or throughout the year as a way to honor their life.

***

Materials: "Mercy Cards"
- Index cards
- Sharpies™

What to Do: For Older Children
1. Give seven index cards to each of your children.
2. Have them write one of the Works of Mercy on each card.
3. Each day, week, or month, fan out your children's cards and have them draw one.
4. Have your children concentrate on that Spiritual Work of Mercy throughout the week.
5. At each evening's supper, have each person share which spiritual work they drew and if they have an example of how that helped them that day.
6. At the end of each week, have your children give you that week's card and draw a new Work of Mercy.
7. Repeat until all the cards have been used or continue it as long as you wish.

***

Materials: "Don't Hesitate"
- A loving and courageous heart

What to Do: For the Family
Remind the family to use the Spiritual Works of Mercy with one other. If they find themselves in a situation that calls for using one of the works of mercy, encourage them not to hesitate. By don't hesitate, we mean to either act right then or if you are unsure how, pray and discern how to best use His work of mercy for help. Never forget the inspiring and at times challenging words of Jesus in Matthew 25:40, "Truly I tell you, just as you did it to one of the least of these who are members of my family, you did it to Me."

***
Prayerful Pause

Dearest Lord,
May we pray for all of Your holy people,
both those who are with us on earth and
those who have gone before us.
Amen.

***
Memos to Me

***
Pondering through Pictures

God the Holy Spirit

***

"The Holy Spirit comes where He is loved, where He is invited, where He is expected."
Saint Bonaventure

I Want You

***

Laurie's Story

"God's Rock Tumbler"

I should start my story by telling you a little something I discovered about my friend, Mary. Long before the bracelets that read, "What would Jesus do?" came out, Mary was asking herself that very question. And she always came up with an answer and didn't hesitate to do it. That's how I concluded that The Spirit knew that if He was to get Mary's attention, He had to be quick because she was a very busy woman.

Through the years, I've learned to take it seriously when Mary says, "I got a pop!" because I've learned that the Holy Spirit speaks to Mary when she is doing the dishes, folding the laundry, or doing other mindless tasks. The way the Spirit speaks to Mary has always made her think that she sounded crazy until one day when I was holding my baby while Mary was loading her dishwasher, and I watched her face change. It was as if someone had just told her something she had never thought of before. And I knew it wasn't me because I hadn't said anything. She turned to me and said, "I just got a pop!" To Mary's delight I answered, "I know, I saw it." She was so excited because I was the first person to see how the Spirit speaks to her. And, I was excited because I finally got to see how God gives her messages. At the time, I remember wishing that Mary would take some time to pray about the messages that He gave her. But, at that time of her life, when God gave Mary a message, she ran with it. Here's a perfect example.

One day, Mary called me and said, the Holy Spirit whispered, "Mary, you're hoarding." I never considered her a hoarder - she always shared with me. So, I said, "Shall we pray about it to see what He wants you to do?" But I was too late. She had already gone through her many bins of kids' clothes. She had lots of bins sorted by size because a number of people gave her their hand-me-downs for her children. I was amazed when she gathered six large black garbage bags of clothes to give to me. I wish you could have seen the look on her face when she handed me the bags and said, "I love doing things for God, look at all these bags. I was hoarding." Mary clearly thought that she had answered the Spirit's call. Until my phone rang again, it was Mary, she was doing her dishes when the Holy Spirit said, "Mary you're not through yet." Mary assumed that God was talking about hoarding things again. I had my doubts and was ready to invite Mary to pray about it, but she already had a plan.

During this time, Mary's mom asked Mary and Aaron to rent her house. She figured that since they were selling their house it would be easier for them to make an offer on a new home if they were not tied to the expense of their old home. That made sense to Mary and Aaron, and they accepted her gracious offer. This decision meant they would have to begin clearing out their basement because Mary's mom's house was smaller than theirs.

So, Mary went to work, answering the Spirit's call by gathering up her basement and carting it over to her neighbor's garage, because her neighbor was going to have a garage sale in a couple of weeks. About a week later, I came up to visit, and we walked over to the neighbor's house to borrow something. The neighbor wanted to show Mary how the sale preparations were going. As I was looking through things, I commented on items that I loved or needed and if it was Mary's item, she would say, "Oh, just take it." I took about ninety percent of Mary's things for my new house. Mary was glad her belongings were going to a good home. Again, she believed that she had answered God's call.

On my next visit up, Mary and I were in her basement when I saw a hanging wardrobe with a few clothes in it and asked her, "Whose clothes are these?" Mary told me that they were beautiful silk suits that her mom had given her for job interviews. Mary laughed and said, "I was thinner in those days and thought I might wear them again someday." A few days later Mary called me and said, "I've been thinking that maybe God wants me to give the suits away too." When I asked her why she thought that Mary told me that she didn't think it was a coincidence that I had pointed the suits out to her at about the same time the Holy Spirit told her that she was hoarding. I invited her to spend some time praying to make sure that that was what God really wanted. But again, Mary had made up her mind. She was going to take her suits to a consignment shop.

So, the next day Mary visited four shops, but not one of them would take her clothes. They either were not taking women's clothes at all, or they would not take items that were more than three years old. It didn't matter if the suits were classic in style or not. That evening, I had a long phone conversation with Mary. She was exasperated with the consignment shops. Mary could not figure out for the life of her why anyone in their right mind would not take such lovely suits.

Once Mary calmed down, I asked her if she would consider praying about it. I thought maybe the consignment shops' refusal to take the suits was God's way of telling Mary that He did not care if she kept them. My offer was met with a heavy sigh followed by a long silence. Again, I was too late because Mary had already given her suits to Goodwill, hoping she'd get a tax receipt.

But the man at Goodwill told her that he did not have any tax receipts to give that day. I couldn't help but giggle when Mary told me the next part. She told me that, "With bowed head, I acknowledged to my Lord, 'You want me to give these away too, don't cha?'"

When it came time for Mary's mom to move out of her house, Aaron and Mary were a big help. As they packed her mom, it became obvious that they would not have enough room in her house for all of their books. They had both saved textbooks from college and many of the books that they had enjoyed reading together through the years. With this realization, Aaron decided that they should go through all of their books and only keep a few important ones. Mary took this as yet another sign from God. I knew that she truly used a lot of her books, so again, I suggested that we pray about it to see if that is really what the Holy Spirit had in mind. Again, I wasn't fast enough; Mary and Aaron had four boxes of books packed up. They had decided to take them to Half Price Books and sell them. I wanted to ask Mary if she was sure about this, but she had already moved on. I still haven't figured out how to keep up with Mary when she puts her hyper-focused ADD mind to something because her body keeps up.

Mary loaded the boxes and packed the kids into the van, and they were off. I still laugh to this day about what Mary said happened next. They were nearly there when Mary rounded the final corner, Half Price Books had burned to the ground. In disbelief, Mary just stared straight ahead, shaking her head, and noticed that a block down the road there stood a Goodwill trailer. Mary says she looked up to heaven, saluted, and said "Yes, Sir."

I think the Holy Spirit popped something into Mary's head that day because she says that right then, she realized that God did not want her stuff, He wanted her. When she got home, Mary called me laughing hysterically as she tried to tell me what had happened. I laughed along with her and when we finally gathered ourselves long enough to catch our breath, I asked her if she wanted to pray about it. That set us back into fits of laughter as she answered, "Yes." And she has been saying yes ever since, although I gotta tell you, God still pops things into Mary's head, it's just not out of necessity anymore.

***

Heavenly Hint

"I shall give them a single heart and I shall put a new Spirit in them; I shall remove their heart of stone..."
Ezekiel 11:19

***

Reflection

Imagine for a moment that you are a formidable rock that lives on a mountaintop. Your texture is rough, and you are jagged around the edges. You have lived on the mountaintop for years, with no plans to move, when suddenly an earthquake hits, shaking you loose and turning you over and over down the mountain and into the rough rapids of a river below. You are now tumbling through the water and banging into other rocks. As you move further and further downriver, it seems that time has stopped. You feel as though these rapid waters will never slow and the pain from the tumbling will never end. However, through it all, you notice that your jagged edges are rounding out.

Suddenly, the river bends, and you come to a standstill. For a moment, the river's cool water comforts you, and you notice that your texture has changed. Another rock bumps into you and again you are on the move. However, the ride is less tumultuous this time. You are able to find some joy in the journey. At long last, you stop in a stream. You hardly recognize your own reflection in the water, for you are no longer that rough and jagged rock, you have changed into a smooth pebble.

When we humble ourselves in prayer, we are like the changing rock as it moves down the river to humbly rest in the stream below. Prayer transforms our hearts. God sends the Holy Spirit to make us new. Just as the river's water transformed the jagged rock into a smooth pebble, the Holy Spirit transforms our stony hearts into humble hearts.

The moral of the story is that sometimes our wills can be as hard as a rock, but if we allow the Spirit to work in our hearts then our wills can become as small as a pebble. While we are building our households of faith, let us turn to the Holy Spirit to provide the wisdom needed to teach our children to do the will of God. Do not make the same mistake Mary made in the above memory. She thought she was acting on the promptings of the Spirit, but she was wrong. So, the Holy Spirit tumbled her like the rock on the mountain until she understood His call. She should have listened to the wise words of St. Faustina, "The soul's true greatness is in loving God and in humbling oneself in His presence..." Mary originally thought that the Spirit was calling her to be charitable. She thought that He was asking her to stop hoarding her possessions. It turned out that what the Holy Spirit wanted was Mary. The Spirit's desire was for Mary to turn to Him in prayer and build a deeper relationship with Him. It took the Holy Spirit to transform Mary's "stony heart" into a heart willing to listen, rather than to guess, the will of God. If Mary had stopped to pray with Laurie, she might not have needed tumbling at all because she would have had a chance to hear what He truly wanted from her, which was her heart.

Moms, if we believe we are hearing the prompting of the Spirit, let us avoid the Holy Spirit's rock tumbler by praying to determine what He is calling us to. Our heart's desire should be one with the Holy Spirit just as Saint Gabriel of the Sorrowful Mother once said, "I will attempt day by day to break my will into pieces. I want to do God's Holy Will, not my own!" As we awaken each morning, may we give ourselves over to the Spirit to lead us and guide us in doing the will of God, the One who loves us.

***
Homework from Heaven

"Sticky Mess"

Materials:
- Two cans of dark-colored pop
- Computer or construction paper
- Tape
- Scissors
- Marker
- Two white kitchen-sized plastic garbage bags

What to Do:
1. Cut out a piece of the paper to wrap around one of the cans. Before taping it in place, write, "Doing the Spirit's Will."
2. Cut out a piece of the paper to wrap around the other can. Before taping it in place, write, "Doing My Will."
3. Take the cans outside where a mess can be made without worries. Lay the white garbage bags down on the ground side by side.
4. Set down one can of pop on each bag.
5. Gather everyone around the can that says, "Doing the Spirit's Will" and be still and quiet for a moment. Slowly open the can. Allow everyone to hear it fizz. Liken this experience to opening your will to the Holy Spirit, then taking the time to listen to Him prayerfully. The Spirit can be this simple if we take the time to listen.
6. Next, gather everyone around the can that says, "Doing My Will" and shake the heck out of it, and then open it, allowing your children to see what happens. Explain that this is the kind of sticky mess we can create when we, like Mary, don't take the time to give ourselves to the Spirit and listen to Him.

✶✶✶
Prayerful Pause

Sweet Spirit,
Please help us to pray and give ourselves to You, thereby saving ourselves a heap load of trouble.
Amen.

***
Memos to Me

_____

_____

_____

_____

_____

_____

_____

_____

***
Pondering through Pictures

Spotlight on the Spirit

***

"The Holy Spirit is the Spirit sent by Christ to carry out in us the work of holiness."
Saint Josemaria Escriva

Holy Help

***

In the following chapters, we will revisit the promise Jesus made to us in John 14:16-17, "I will ask the Father, and He will give you another Advocate, to be with you forever. This is the Spirit of Truth... You know Him, because He abides with you, and He will be in you." This Spirit of Truth is the Holy Spirit and He has seven gifts to help us. He offers us His gifts of wisdom, understanding, knowledge, counsel, fortitude, piety, and fear of the Lord. As we accept these gifts, God's grace can flow through our hearts and the hearts of our family.

It is imperative that we not only teach our children these gifts but also teach them to turn to the Holy Spirit for His guidance. So, we will discuss and accept the gifts that our Advocate wants to give us. Let us have a look at the power of the Holy Spirit and His seven gifts.

Gifts of the Holy Spirit

***
Wisdom
Understanding
Knowledge
Counsel
Fortitude
Piety
Fear of the Lord

We Accept It

***

Mary's Memory

"Kingdom of God"

When Patrick was in eighth grade, he had a religion teacher who taught the importance of loving and serving God. He often discussed spreading the Kingdom of God by loving people through community service. He even presented ways for his students to accomplish this. His class was particularly good about helping younger students. It was such a wonderful way to bring God's presence to the school community.

Patrick's teacher had a motto to help his students remember the importance of this valuable lesson. When they graduated from eighth grade, he told his students to go out and "Spread the KOG." This meant to go out and spread the Kingdom of God wherever and to whomever you can.

***

Heavenly Hint

"By wisdom a house is built..."
Proverbs 24:3

***

Reflection

The first Gift of the Holy Spirit is wisdom. Wisdom helps us to keep our hearts and minds focused on God. Pope Francis said, "It is the action of the Holy Spirit which gives us wisdom... Let us allow the Spirit to lead us forward in that wisdom, which is like a soft breeze. This is the Spirit of the Kingdom of God, of which Jesus speaks." When we keep our focus on the Spirit's call, we bring the Kingdom of God right here on earth. As we center our lives on the Holy Spirit, we follow Jesus' command to love one another as God first loved us. This command is what Patrick's teacher was talking about in Mary's memory. He was encouraging his students to love others, not because the person loves them, but because this will "Spread the KOG" and bring God's love to other people.

    As the students do community service, they learn to ask for the Holy Spirit's gift of wisdom. God can help them determine what His plan is for their lives. As they do a variety of community service, they see what sparks their interest and what their strengths are. If we teach our children to ask for the Spirit's wisdom as they go, then He will lovingly guide them on their journey. Wisdom is what empowers us to determine our steps. God has a plan for each of our lives, and as the third Person of God, the Holy Spirit knows that plan well. When we pray for the gift of wisdom, we are best able to learn it and live it.

    Wisdom is imperative in our lives. Equipped with the Spirit's gift of wisdom and prayerful discernment of God's plan for our families, we can bring the Kingdom of God to our children's lives, for not only at the center of wisdom is God's plan but also God's love. As we, like Patrick's teacher, love our children and teach them to love others, we are instructing them about the nature of God, for God is love. When we teach our children to love others, we teach them to center on God's will or plan, which we know in part is to spread the Kingdom of God right here on earth. We simply do not know how or what God has uniquely planned for our children, and neither do they. But teaching our children to ask for the Holy Spirit's gift of wisdom in their lives will undoubtedly help them to discern that plan. Moms, let us embrace the Holy Spirit's gift of wisdom and teach our children to do the same by loving others and "Spreading the KOG" to those around us.

***

Homework from Heaven

"Spread the KOG"

What to Do:

"Spread the KOG" in your neighborhood. It's a great place to start your efforts. Here are a few ideas to get you rolling:

1. Buy cards for your neighbors on the next holiday. Let them know you are glad they are your neighbors and that you enjoy them being in your life.
2. Introduce yourself to some neighbors you have not yet met.
3. Initiate a block party, so everyone can get to know each other better.
4. Invite the neighbors to the next big game.
5. Next time you see a neighbor doing a big job, offer to help.
6. Initiate a neighborhood garage sale.
7. Don't hesitate to "Spread the KOG!"

***

Prayerful Pause

Dear Holy Spirit,
Thank you for Your gift of wisdom.
We accept it.
Amen.

***
Memos to Me

_____

_____

_____

_____

_____

_____

_____

***
Pondering through Pictures

Child-Smart/God-Smart

***

Mary's Memory

"Now Prepared for God's Call"
(Kathleen's High School Religion Paper)

My life has been met with unique blessings and difficulties from the beginning. These difficulties have taught me to do what God requires of me, "...to act justly, love tenderly and walk humbly with your God." (Micah 6:8) I was diagnosed with apraxia a couple of months before I turned two. My apraxia was developmental, which meant I did not have to live with it forever, but it did present both physical and intellectual issues. I learned to be patient with both myself and others because of it. The apraxia humbled me and made me grow up faster. It taught me to treat people justly, it taught me to love people regardless of our differences, and it definitely taught me to walk humbly with God.

My mom tells me that fostering my physical and intellectual development required also having a strong faith. She says it was both a job and a joy. I had apraxia from birth to fourth grade. That means all the language and information learned was in my mind but there was a disconnect from my brain to my mouth, as well as from my brain to my arm. I guess I was frustrated a lot. My folks took me to speech therapy from twenty-two months to almost four years in order to reroute my brain and get me speaking. Then, they had to help me to write. Again, the information was in my mind, but it had to be rerouted for me to get it down on paper. That meant spending three years in a special program at a local public elementary school. I loved my teacher - she was so good to me. My teacher was just one of many blessings along my apraxia journey.

Mom and Dad had to spend lots of extra time at home with

me too. They were constantly helping me to put my thoughts together, so that they all made sense. We played lots of development learning games, and my mom even made a book identical to the one my speech therapist had to use with me at home. With all this effort being put into apraxia, my folks tell me they worried about my spiritual development getting lost in the shuffle. That's part of why they sent me to a Catholic school. It was a major challenge for the first several years. My mom didn't let that stop me though. She drove me to the public school after lunch every day so that I could work with the teacher I loved so much. Mom was always doing activities with me that taught me about faith too. I thought that was typical in every family. I have since figured out that this was her way of building my faith while helping with my apraxia. The God that I grew up with is a God of love and compassion. He gave me people in my life that I could rely on to help me get past my struggles.

Once I began fifth grade, I had to rethink my abilities. I was no longer struggling and found it strange as I competed against my friends because I was no longer at a deficit. I had become accustomed to failing in most challenges when compared to my friends and was used to my mom and dad encouraging me to be patient. They'd tell me that I was just as smart but just needed more time. It was weird to me because suddenly they were saying things like, "Shine Kathleen, and believe in yourself." They told me that I had to start talking differently to myself because I was no longer at a deficit.

Affirmations had to be given regularly on all the little things as well as the big to change my thinking. Mom tells me that what was amazing to her, is that given everything I just described, I always had a smile on my face. She called me her joyful spirit. While I still struggle with my self-talk and my abilities, I know that God has provided me with all that I need and will eventually get me to a place where I believe in myself as long as I always strive to do His will.

Now, I'm prepared and able to move forward in life and achieve whatever God calls me to. These experiences have made me both strong and compassionate. I've been told that I am wise beyond my years. I do not know if that is true, but I do know how important a relationship with God is. I have relied on His love and mercy my entire life.

***

Heavenly Hint

*"By wisdom a house is built,
by understanding it is made strong..."*
Proverbs 24:3

***

Reflection

  The second gift of the Holy Spirit is understanding. This gift of understanding helps us to emulate Jesus, which will take becoming both child-smart and God-smart. Jesus was masterful at both, and not only was He a great communicator, but He also accepted people where they were at. Accepting people where they are at is a loving way to carry out our faith. The Holy Spirit understands how to help us effectively love like Jesus did when He was on earth.

  Becoming child-smart will take learning what our children need and studying the developmental stages to understand them better as they grow and change. Moms will need to recognize that each of their children is unique and that they will need the Holy Spirit's gift of understanding to help them guide each child's growth in self-love and self-acceptance.

  One big way to get child-smart is to model Jesus and learn how to be a great communicator with our children by doing as Jesus did and accepting our children where they are at. Mary had to do that with Kathleen in her above memory. The untold part of Kathleen's religion paper is that the doctors informed Mary that Kathleen was fine and that she was simply slow to talk. Mary's instinct countered that assessment, which required Mary to call on the Spirit's help to understand what Kathleen needed. If she had not trusted her instinct and turned to the Spirit, Kathleen would likely be mute today because she needed her brain rerouted while young in order to overcome her developmental apraxia.

Equipped with the Holy Spirit's understanding, Mary both intently and actively "listened" to Kathleen, at first through her actions because she struggled to talk, until she was about four. Mary had to often practice active listening because Mary had to guess what Kathleen was trying to tell her through her actions. This active listening required taking the time to ask many questions and watch Kathleen's body language to understand her need or want. This mode of communication took place until Kathleen could finally talk for herself. However, just because Kathleen learned to speak, Mary's active listening did not stop there. However, it changed.

We moms can actively listen to our children too. This form of listening requires telling our children our understanding of what they said, in order to confirm that we get it. Active listening is used when we want to clarify what was said to us rather than assume what was said to us because assuming can get us in trouble. We need to explain the process of active listening to our children so that they understand why we are repeating them. The Spirit's gift of understanding can help this process because the Spirit will help us to truly understand what our children are saying to us. Active listening in particular, is a critical piece of communication. When this piece of communication is left out, misunderstandings can happen. It is vital to both model and teach active listening.

As we teach our children how to live their faith, we ought to teach them the value of communication by first being open to the Holy Spirit and then listening to the people around them, for we learn when we listen. So let us teach our children to listen to other people actively and to capitalize on the Holy Spirit's gift of understanding.

Now, we will discuss how asking for the Spirit's gift of understanding will help us to be God-smart. We will need His gift of understanding to learn the things of God. Being God-smart recognizes that God has many ways of helping us. We must stay open to our options, for some options are opportunities that God is placing before us. It will also take listening to God. As moms, we do not always have a lot of time in our day. However, we have to make the time to listen to our Holy Counselor. We can do it in the car, or while doing mindless tasks like folding laundry or doing the dishes. Listening simply requires opening our hearts to the Spirit. He will do the rest. Do not get frustrated. Sometimes, it takes time to hear or see the opportunities the Holy Spirit is presenting. The Spirit will never give up on us, and we must not give up on Him. As Saint Dorotheos of Gaza explained to us, "In the measure that we pay attention and take care to carry out what we hear, God will always enlighten us and help us to understand."

Moms, commit to allowing the Holy Spirit to help us to become both child-smart and God-smart. May we never stop growing in both of these important endeavors. As we seek to become more child-smart and God-smart, let us remember to keep the Holy Spirit at the center of it all by asking for His gift of understanding.

***

Homework from Heaven

"What's Fair?"

What to Do:
1. Part of being child-smart is paying attention to the uniqueness of each of your children. What one child needs another might not. They are individuals. Often, it is a child's instinct to want things to be fair, meaning being treated the same and getting the same things. Consider teaching your children a different definition of the word fair. Explain that being fair means giving each child what they need, rather than giving all the children the same thing. For example, one child might like playing lacrosse and another might devour books. Do you have to be fair

and spend the same amount of money on lacrosse and books? No, you supply what each child needs in the way they need it. The lacrosse equipment costs more than books, especially if you introduce your child to a library. Being fair might mean encouraging and watching one child's lacrosse games while at the same time encouraging the other child's love of reading by sitting down and reading with them.

2. Part of being God-smart is teaching our children that God always provides for our needs. Don't allow your children to compare what their friends have to what they have. Fairness applies to that as well. Teach your children that it is okay if they have more than someone else. They can always share. Or that it is okay if someone else has more than them. It's important to be content with what you have and with what you have been given. Knowing this comes with listening to the Spirit's gift of understanding.

***

Prayerful Pause

Dear Holy Spirit,
Thank you for Your gift of understanding.
We accept it.
Amen.

***
Memos to Me

_____
_____
_____
_____
_____
_____
_____

***
Pondering through Pictures

Matters of the Heart

***

Laurie's Story

"Teaching Jonathan"

Steve and I decided to homeschool Jonathan the summer before he went into sixth grade. I was eager to get started, so I contacted my sister-in-law who homeschools her son. Our sons are the same age. When we got together, she laid out all of the curriculum she uses and let me go through it. As I went through it, she explained why she chose each curriculum. It all made sense to me, so I went with it. She then offered to plug Jonathan and me into many of the same co-ops that she was a part of. We were set and I was so grateful!

Teaching Jonathan has been a joy. Studying geography together has been a treat, quite literally. We make food from the different cultures of the world. Studying the lives of the saints has been wonderful because they inspire us to love God and others more. It's been fun to find the saints that we are studying show up in our world history book. We like reading the stories of history, they fascinate us. Which leads us to the study of our faith. It's been a gift to both teach and learn about God and our faith together.

***

Heavenly Hint

*"By wisdom a house is built,
by understanding it is made strong;
by knowledge its storerooms are filled with
riches of every kind, rare and desirable."
Proverbs 24:3-4*

***

Reflection

The third gift of the Holy Spirit is knowledge. Knowledge is gaining information about God's truth. We will have to continue to gain knowledge to teach our children. We must be lifelong learners studying, learning, and growing along with our children. It is also necessary to know what Aristotle once said, "Educating the mind without educating the heart is no education at all." So, moms, we will need to provide ongoing knowledge about the truths of our faith, for they are matters of the heart.

With the guidance of the Holy Spirit's gift of knowledge, we are better able to make sound judgments. In Laurie's story above, it was definitely a sound decision to homeschool Jonathan. Referencing back to the Heavenly Hint, Laurie's home is "filled with riches of every kind, rare and desirable." Laurie's heart is full as she teaches her son the faith. She is confident that he is learning God's truth as they read and discuss the faith together.

It is our responsibility as moms to teach our children to ask for and accept the gift of knowledge that the Spirit freely offers. Equipped with this gift, our children will better learn God's truth. With the aid of the Holy Spirit, learning about and discerning the truth of God will be easier, for our children are not left to worldly understanding - they have their Advocate helping them.

Moms, we will need to both model and teach our children to actively pursue the Holy Spirit and His gift of knowledge. This pursuit will take asking for the Holy Spirit's gift of knowledge throughout our lives. Moms, let us continue to learn God's truth, for if we are not lifelong learners, we will become stagnant. Then, we risk stifling our children, for they will indeed imitate our behavior and stop learning themselves. So, stay hungry for knowledge about the faith. Let our children see our hunger, knowing we can count on the Holy Spirit to be there with His wonderful gift of knowledge.

***

Homework from Heaven
"On Shaky Ground"

Materials:
- A ball that your child can stand on with help
- A sturdy box or something similar that your child can safely stand on

What to Do:
Laurie's decision to homeschool Jonathan is laying a solid foundation for Jonathan's faith. As moms it's important we actively participate in teaching our children about God. If we don't we run the risk of our children learning what the world will tell them.

1. Have your child try to stand on the ball. Choose balls that will challenge older children. Of course, stay close so that they don't fall.
2. Ask your child if it is easy to stand on the ball. When they say no, explain that that is because they are standing on shaky ground.

3. Tell your children that without God's truth, they are indeed on shaky ground, because the world will tell them what they want to hear, regardless of whether or not it is correct.

In Contrast:
1. Have your child stand on the box.
2. Ask your child if it is easy to stand on the box. When they say yes, explain that that is because they are standing on stable ground.
3. Tell your children that with God's Truth, they are on stable ground because the Holy Spirit will tell them what they need to know. That is what the gift of the Holy Spirit is all about - He provides us with the knowledge He knows we will need throughout our lives.

***

Prayerful Pause

Sweet Spirit,
Thank You for Your gift of knowledge.
We accept it.
Amen.

***
Memos to Me

_____
_____
_____
_____
_____
_____
_____

***
Pondering through Pictures

Soar Like Eagles

***
Mary's Story
"You're Only Hurting Yourself"

When Maggie was a young adult, she came home for a visit. An event in Maggie's life from a couple years past, came up in conversation. It was about a time that someone had not only made her mad but hurt her. She got aggravated and told me that she is still mad about it. I thought for a moment then told Maggie it might help to stop holding on to that anger and instead forgive the person. She responded that she has already forgiven the person, but when she remembers it, it still makes her mad. I explained that some events in life affect us so deeply that each remembrance of them requires us to forgive again. If we don't, we are only hurting ourselves. It is in forgiveness that we will find healing and the anger and hurt will slip away in time. Maggie nodded and said she'd think about that.

***
Heavenly Hint
"He heals the brokenhearted, and binds up their wounds."
Psalm 147:3

***
Reflection

Counsel is the fourth gift bestowed by the Holy Spirit. To counsel someone means to guide them. Saint Josemaria Escriva said, "Don't fly like a barnyard hen, when you can soar like an eagle." She has a great point. In the story above, Mary guided Maggie when Maggie told her she was still angry about something she had already forgiven someone for. Mary recognized that Maggie's anger had her stuck like the barnyard hen trying to fly with clipped wings. By holding on to that anger, Maggie is hurting herself over and over with each remembrance of the event.

Often, the deeper we have been hurt the longer the anger lasts. However, if we ask for the Spirit's counsel, help is on its way. What's more, when we turn to the Spirit for His gift of counsel, He will help us to soar like eagles. Sometimes we're hurt so deeply that forgiving one time isn't enough. The Spirit will guide us to forgive over and over again every time we remember the person or people that hurt us. Each time we forgive, the person we're taking care of is ourselves knowing that the person that hurt us has likely moved on. The Spirit will help us to let love become bigger than anger and hurt and we will eventually heal. Once healed, we will become unstuck and rather than flying like barnyard hens with clipped wings, we will soar like eagles and spread God's love anew.

***
Homework from Heaven

"Finding Forgiveness"

What to Do:
1. Like Maggie, is there an event that every time you remember it you become angry and hurt again? Try calling on the Spirit's counsel for help and working on forgiveness

at each remembrance. Let the Spirit guide you toward a bigger love so that you can soar like an eagle.
2. Do you know of an event in your child's life that stirs these feelings? Counsel them to do the same.

***

Prayerful Pause

*Spirit of God,
Thank You for Your gift of counsel.
We accept it.
Amen.*

*** Memos to Me

*** Pondering through Pictures

Staying Power

***

Laurie's Story

"Hunger Retreat"

Each year, our youth group attends a two-day Hunger Retreat, where churches from all around the area gather together to appreciate what they have and to give to others in need. The youth and adults at the retreat go without food for twenty-four hours, in order to experience a small taste of what it feels like to go hungry.

On the second day of the retreat, the leader divides everyone into groups and sends them out to serve in various ways. Steve, Sam, Amy, and Rose have all attended this retreat for several years. They would come home and tell me all about it.

Through the years, they have organized food at Saint Vincent de Paul, cleaned up cemeteries, and gone to domestic violence shelters to help the residents organize their belongings. When they went to the nursing homes to hang out with the elderly, Amy and Rose especially liked painting the ladies' nails, because the ladies would feel so pretty. It clearly brought them joy, and Amy and Rose loved that.

***

Heavenly Hint

"Let us not become weary in doing good, for at the proper time we will reap a harvest if we do not give up."
Galatians 6:9

***
Reflection

The fifth gift of the Holy Spirit is fortitude. Fortitude is necessary for the staying power required for a lifetime of mothering. God's gift of fortitude enables mothers to be steadfast in their vocation with a loving heart. God is always faithful to a mom who takes advantage of the Holy Spirit's gift of fortitude.

The Spirit does this for our children as well. The world barrages our children with messages to "do their own thing" or to "do what feels good." However, the gift of fortitude strengthens them to consistently pursue what is good in the eyes of God, which is to help those around them. In the story above Steve helped his children in this pursuit as together they served their greater community's various needs. It is not always easy to come face to face with the difficulties people in the greater community deal with on a daily basis. The retreat Laurie's children went on exposed them to some of these difficulties. It will take fortitude to continue to say yes. Steve and Laurie provided their children with the opportunity to pursue what is good in the eyes of God, hoping their children will continue this pursuit for a lifetime.

The beautiful thing about this story is that Laurie's family has taken advantage of retreats from generation to generation. They have lived what it says in 2 Timothy 1:5, "I am reminded of your sincere faith, a faith that lived first in your grandmother Lois and your mother Eunice and now, I am sure, lives in you." Laurie's grandmother went on retreats as did Laurie's mom who also went on numerous retreats throughout her life. Laurie too, has been on many retreats. Now, Laurie is bringing this tradition to her family in hopes that her children will carry the lessons learned from their retreats into their lives and maybe one day into the lives of their households of faith.

Saint Francis de Sales once remarked, "The lives of the saints are nothing, but the Gospel put into practice." As we strive to help our children become saints, by pursuing what is good in the eyes of God, they will be putting the Gospel into practice. Putting the Gospel into practice will indeed take fortitude. The Holy Spirit's gift of fortitude is such a powerful gift for our families' ability to stay close to God and to be able to live a life of faith.

***

Homework from Heaven

"What's Good in the Eyes of God"

What to Do:

1. Read this poem by Paul Gilbert to your children:

   "You are writing a Gospel, a chapter each day,
   by deeds that you do, by words that you say.
   Men read what you write, whether faithless or
   true; say, what is the Gospel according to you?"

2. After you have read it to your children, talk about it. Ask your children these questions:

   a. What do you think the poet is trying to say?
   b. If there is no pencil or pen in the poem, how is someone writing something about the gospel?
   c. What is the gospel according to you? How does the poem help you determine it?

3. Perhaps write the poem out and hang it on your refrigerator as a reminder to pursue what is good in God's eyes.

***
Prayerful Pause

*Spirit of Love,
Thank You for Your gift of fortitude.
We accept it.
Amen.*

***
Memos to Me

_____

_____

_____

_____

_____

_____

_____

***
Pondering through Pictures

Devotion

***

Laurie's Story

"Stepping Up"

Seven out of my eight children have struggled with anxiety in one way or another. Some struggled when they were young and grew out of it. Others have struggled into their adulthood. They did not have anxiety one at a time. There were days when several of my children were on the struggle bus at the same time. They all needed me to be there for them. I had to be available to help them feel secure, to help them know that even though they didn't feel safe, they were.

It was beautiful to watch how my children were there for each other. It helped me too, because there were times when two people might need me, but I couldn't be there for both of them at the same time. Another one of the children would step up. There were times when I could not leave the house. So, the kids would support one another by going to each other's soccer games when I couldn't be there to cheer them on. Or the older kids drove the younger kids to their various activities. They also used their own experiences of dealing with anxiety to comfort their siblings and teach them ways to cope. Their compassion and devotion to each other was inspiring.

***

Heavenly Hint

"If one member suffers, all suffer together; if one member is honored, all rejoice together."
1 Corinthians 12:26

***

Reflection

Piety is the sixth gift of the Holy Spirit. Piety is devotion to God. Through His gift of piety, the Holy Spirit provides eagerness for both our children and us as mothers to tell our Lord how very much we love Him, to praise Him for His glory, and to thank Him for His blessings every single day.

One of those blessings is each unique member of our family. As important as it is to have piety for our Lord, it is also important to have faithful love and devotion to one another. In Psalm 133:1 it tells us, "How very good and pleasant it is when kindred live together in unity!" A family should do that. Laurie's story above demonstrates this beautifully. Her children were there for each other when they needed it most. They loved each other through anxiety over and over again. They heard the Holy Spirit calling them to His gift of piety by loving Him, through loving each other.

We need people here on earth who accept and love us for exactly how God made us. Mr. Rogers, from the most beautiful neighborhood on earth, once said, "Love isn't a state of perfect caring. It is an active noun like struggle. To love someone is to strive to accept that person exactly the way they are, right here and now." Family devotion includes that. Part of piety within a family does mean supporting each other as Laurie's children did, but it is also important to take time to pray, play, and be together. Spending time together as a family helps to strengthen family bonds and provides opportunities to become closer to one another. Every child needs to know that they can count on their family for that kind of love.

***

Homework from Heaven

"Penny Prayer"/ "Family Devotion"

Materials: "Penny Prayer"
- A penny on the ground
- A prayerful heart

What to Do: For All Ages"
1. Whenever one of your children finds a penny on the ground, teach them to pick it up and then say, "Find a penny, say a prayer, knowing that God's always there." Then, tell them to say their prayer. Remind your children that it doesn't matter what they pray. What matters is that they lift to the Lord whatever is in their hearts.
2. Have your children say this rhyme in the same sing-song way as the "traditional" [8]penny pick-up rhyme: "Find a penny, pick it up, all day long, you'll have good luck."
3. The beauty of the new rhyme is that it leads our children to prayer.

***

What to Do: "Family Devotion"
1. Keep an eye out for times you can affirm, reinforce, and encourage your children to show respect and love toward each other.
2. Help your children to "Spread the KOG" right at home. As in Laurie's story, encourage your children to accept and

support each other right where they're at. In this way, we honor the dignity and worth of each person as unique children of God and members of our family.

***

Prayerful Pause

*Dear Holy Spirit,
Thank You for Your gift of piety.
We accept it.
Amen.*

***
Memos to Me

_____
_____
_____
_____
_____
_____
_____
_____

***
Pondering through Pictures

Reverence & Awe

***

Mary's Memory

"Flying High"

It was my sophomore year in college and my boyfriend, who wasn't Aaron because I hadn't met him yet, had earned his pilot's license. He wanted to take me on a romantic date, so he took me up to fly over Pullman, Washington. It was beautiful! Afterward, he took me to an Italian restaurant. It was a lovely evening.

The next day, I saw my brother Jim and some of his friends. I was still happy about the evening before and told him all about it. To my surprise, he responded, "You did what?! Dad's going to be livid!" I looked at him, puzzled, and said, "What? Why?" Jim asked how many hours my boyfriend had in the air, and I told him a little over a hundred. It seemed like a lot to me. Jim explained that for a pilot to earn a license, they have to have a minimum of one hundred hours in the air. I sunk! - I knew Jim was right. Dad would be both mad and disappointed in me.

I went back to my dorm room and thought about what I should do. I could not tell my dad, but then again, Jim might or one of his friends. That would disappoint Dad even more. I couldn't stand the thought of that, so I decided to call home and face the music. While my dad was mad and disappointed, he thanked me for telling him myself. He accepted that I did not understand the situation and made me promise not to go up with my boyfriend again. I agreed. In the end, I was glad I told him myself. I knew it was essential to give my dad that much respect.

***
Heavenly Hint

*"Is not your fear of God
your confidence, and the integrity
of your ways, your hope?"*
Job 4:6

***

Reflection

    The seventh and final gift of the Holy Spirit is fear of the Lord. God is awesome. "Awe" means to worship and revere - our fear comes from the knowledge of God's awesome greatness. Fear of the Lord should first acknowledge that God deserves our respect, for God is our Creator, the source of all life, a Creator who loves us and wants what's best for us. To help us achieve this, Deuteronomy 10:12-13 tells us, "So now, O Israel, what does the Lord your God require of you? Only to fear the Lord your God, to walk in all his ways, to love him, to serve the Lord your God with all your heart and with all your soul, and to keep the commandments of the Lord your God and his decrees that I am commanding you today, for your own well-being." As children of God, we should primarily fear hurting our relationship with Him, much like a child's fear of disappointing their father for a father wants the well-being of his children.

    The risk of disappointment was the fear that Mary had for her dad in the memory above. After talking to her brother Jim, Mary understood that her decision would disappoint her dad because she put herself in a potentially unsafe situation. Mary's dad loved her and made it clear that he only wanted what was best for her throughout her lifetime. This demonstration of God's love created the basis for Mary loving her dad. She could not stand the thought of disappointing or hurting her dad and, therefore, breaking the trust between them. Instead, Mary revered her father by explaining what she had done, rather than risking him hearing it from her brother or one of his friends. While she did not intend to hurt her father, once her brother Jim explained it to Mary, she knew that out of love and respect for her dad, she had to tell him herself. Mary's desire not to disappoint her father came out of the knowledge of his constant love for her.

The Holy Spirit's gift of Fear of the Lord develops a sincere desire to revere God. Saint Francis de Sales explained it perfectly when he said, "We must fear God out of love, not love Him out of fear." Let us teach our children the importance of fearing the Lord and help them to love God with such fervor that they would never choose to risk compromising their relationship with Him and disappointing Him. Moms, let us help our children to truly know how deeply God loves them and that His love is constant.

***

Homework from Heaven

"God's Awesome Greatness"

What to Do:
1. Gather your family together.
2. Brainstorm different words that describe what it means to fear the Lord. For example: worship, respect, awe, reverence, or desire to please.
3. Break into groups.
4. Give each group a word that the family agrees describes fearing the Lord. Have each group create a skit or describe a situation showing how a person can demonstrate fearing the Lord in the right way and in the wrong way. Here are two examples:
    a. Awe - We're standing in front of the ocean. Do we take a moment to marvel at the greatness of God

and praise Him for His glory, or do we complain that the water is too cold and that we could step on a jellyfish?
   b. Respect - We're leaving the church after Mass. Do we take the bulletin from the usher and run? Or, do we take the bulletin and then take the time to greet the priest by thanking him and wishing him a great week ahead?

5. Discuss each outcome and how it shows or fails to show, Fear of the Lord.
6. Make sure they know that the skit or the situation described can be directed toward God or toward someone on earth as was the case in Mary's memory.

***

Prayerful Pause

Precious Spirit,
Thank You for Your gift
of fear of the Lord.
We accept it.
Amen.

*** Memos to Me

*** Pondering through Pictures

Seven Gifts and a Friend

***

Mary's Memory

"Panic"

Laurie's world began falling apart at what should have been one of the happiest times of her life because it was one month before her wedding. However, Laurie became anxious and withdrew into herself. Fear consumed her thoughts as she envisioned being up on the altar in front of so many people, with no escape. All the stress of putting the wedding together began to take its toll. I began to worry when Laurie told me that she had lost eleven pounds because she did not have eleven pounds to lose.

I wanted to support her during this time of struggle. Laurie began telling me that she often felt faint, that her heart kept racing, and that she feared she would die. I asked myself, "What is wrong with her?" But, when I communicated my concern, she'd tell me that she was just nervous about the wedding and that she would be fine when it was over. I had my doubts but went with it because I did not want to be a source of further stress.

Laurie's spring wedding came and went, but her feelings of anxiety stayed. That summer, Laurie would have sudden feelings of terror hit her that would come out of nowhere. She had times of feeling shortness of breath, times of hyperventilating, as well as times of heart palpitations. While Laurie was looking forward to teaching again because she loved being with the kids, she also felt a sense of dread.

As the summer was drawing to a close and we were getting ready to start teaching school again, Laurie told me that the thought of it made her feel awful all over. She was afraid of being out of control while in the classroom. She knew she couldn't leave because she was the adult in charge, and just the idea of it made her feel stuck, like a person in an elevator who has claustrophobia. Laurie asked me, "How much worse will my anxiety be when I'm actually there?" I didn't have a good answer. I felt helpless.

Laurie started the school year, but by October, she had to stop teaching for health reasons. Laurie's anxiety completely overwhelmed her, rendering her unable to teach. It was then that I knew Laurie needed medical intervention. I began asking questions. Questioning her made her uncomfortable and increased her anxiety, but Laurie didn't tell me this. Instead, Laurie gave me the good news that she was pregnant. She turned her attention to being pregnant because she figured the pregnancy was causing her anxiety. I was struggling to get Laurie to see the benefits of medical help. So, I continued to pray with her. We prayed our hearts out, primarily for supernatural healing, though little did Laurie know, I was praying for her to get medical help as well.

Laurie continued to seek help by attending healing services, reading books, and seeking help from counselors, but there was no resolution to her feelings of terror. One day, Laurie called to tell me that she had spent the night in the emergency room because she thought she was having a heart attack. The doctors found nothing wrong with her heart. At this point, I knew that I had to risk getting tough. I insisted that Laurie get herself to a doctor. Thankfully, she was finally desperate enough to acquiesce. The first doctor that Laurie saw referred her for a Magnetic Resonance Imaging scan (MRI). The idea of this terrified Laurie.

Through the years, Laurie and I have jokingly called each other "Laurel and Marty" because goofy, unexpected things just seem to happen when we are together, and the next part demonstrates this, even when Laurie's level of anxiety is extreme. I remember going to the Imaging Center with Laurie to get her MRI because she was not only reluctant but, in her fear, flat out refused to go alone, and Steve could not go with her. Getting Laurie through that MRI was the most interesting rosary we've ever prayed.

When we got there, the technicians offered Laurie medication to calm her down. Instead, Laurie asked if I would come into the MRI with her and pray a rosary. She hoped it would keep her calm. So, being the take-action gal, I talked them into allowing me to go into the room with her. I might not have, had I known in advance what was going to happen next. You see, Laurie is claustrophobic, and the thought of going into a long tube was terrifying, so Laurie grabbed my hand and began leading us in the Joyful Mysteries. The technician pressed the button that started Laurie moving into the tube. Laurie looked at me with panicked eyes and tightened her grip as the technician requested me to let go of Laurie's hand. I looked at the technician and said, "It's not me that needs to let go," as I was forced to walk closer and closer to the opening of the tube. The technician looked stunned as my arm went into the tube with Laurie, and I found myself pressed up against the machine. Laurie discovered that the technicians could talk to her through a two-way speaker inside the tube. The technicians asked if Laurie was okay. She said, "NO!" Then they said, "You need to let go of your friend's hand." Laurie responded, "NO!" I looked up at the technicians in the control room above and said, "What do I do?" They decided it wasn't hindering the pictures, so they went with it.

Once they turned the machine on, I could not hear Laurie. Apparently, during the test, one of the technicians asked Laurie if she was okay, and she told him that she needed me to speak up. As the technician relayed that Laurie needed me to speak louder, he openly laughed at me. I must have been a sight as I squatted with my face pressed against the machine and my arm stretched inside, holding Laurie's hand. If that was not enough, I was literally shouting the rosary, so Laurie could hear me over the noise of the machine. But I didn't care because my focus was on my friend. To Laurie's relief and mine, the technicians decided to end the test early because they thought they had gotten enough pictures. To this day, I believe it was at Mother Mary's prodding. She knew that neither one of us could handle the situation much longer. Laurie had test after test, but the answers were all the same. Nothing was wrong. Our questions were not getting answered.

After Laurie told a couple of friends about the MRI fiasco, one of them suggested that Laurie take medication for help. I knew that she couldn't bring herself to do it. She had told me a zillion times that she was too scared of any side effects. That, I could refute. But it took me a long time to figure out her ultimate reason for refusing to consider medication. Laurie was afraid that by taking medicine, she would be turning her back on God because she knew that he could heal her in the blink of an eye. Laurie believed that either God would answer her prayers and heal her or that she could find a way to overcome the anxiety on her own.

You see, Laurie had discovered that when she turned to the medical community for help, it increased her panic; consequently, she did not do anything beyond having tests done. Once I figured this out, I knew that I was going to have to turn the very God that Laurie relied on "against her." This aha moment broke my heart, but I acted anyway.

I sought Divine intervention by pouring over the Bible. Alleluia, I found something in the book of Sirach 38:1-2,4, "Honor physicians for their services, for the Lord created them; for their gift of healing comes from the Most High... The Lord created medicines out of the earth, and the sensible will not despise them." This scripture helped me figure out how to tell Laurie what she was doing. "You have had a lot of tests to find out what is wrong, but you have never taken that final step the doctors need you to if it means giving up control by taking medicine, despite your fear." She knew I was right, so before she lost her nerve, Laurie got up and called the specialist her doctor had repeatedly asked her to see and made an appointment. That was our first miracle! The specialist quickly diagnosed Laurie with a panic disorder and prescribed medication. "Uh-Oh!" I thought, if Laurie was going to follow through this time, we were in for weeks of major prayer sessions, but to my delight, despite her near paralyzing fear, Laurie did it. She took the medicine immediately! Our second miracle!

After six long years of suffering, Laurie improved with only one week on medication. After a month of medication, she was back! Our greatest miracle! When I asked Laurie how she got herself to take the medicine so quickly, she answered, "I had to do it quickly before I chickened out." We both laughed, and I gave her a great big hug. By taking that medicine, Laurie was not turning her back on God. Quite the opposite, she had to so wholly rely on Him that in the end, Laurie's faith gave her the strength it took to act on how God chose to help her.

***

Heavenly Hint

"Since we are living by the Spirit, let our behavior be guided by the Spirit... So then, as long as we have the opportunity let all our actions be for the good of everybody, and especially of those who belong to the household of the faith."
Galatians 5:25 & 6:10

***

Reflection

In Laurie's story above, it took each gift of the Holy Spirit to help her. Not because she was ignoring God, but because she was so anxiety-riddled that she was struggling to hear Him. Laurie prayed consistently and focused on God. However, her focus was on her request to end her anxiety. She could not hear the Holy Spirit's gift of wisdom telling her, "I want to help you, but I need you to do your part. I need you to trust Me enough to act." But Laurie wanted a miraculous healing by God alone.

Mary tried over and over to help Laurie understand that going to the doctor might help her anxiety, but Laurie was determined to solve her anxiety in her own way. Her greatest desire was for a miracle. Laurie could not hear the Spirit's gift of understanding if it took her out of her comfort zone. At that time, she thought that she could overcome her anxiety on her own, so she read books about diet, went on healing retreats, and never stopped praying. God knew what she needed to do, yet she focused singularly on potential solutions she could control.

Asking for the Holy Spirit's gift of knowledge and opening herself up to Him may have resolved her anxiety sooner because it would have led her to take the medication that He knew would help her. However, Laurie feared the side effects of medication, and it prevented her from taking action. Eventually, Laurie did go to several doctors, but it did not help her because she did not heed their advice. Her plight was similar to that of the man in The Parable of the Flood. Here is the story:

> [9]"A terrible storm descends on a country town. Eventually the streets are flooded, and the water is rising fast. The town preacher is standing on the steps of the church, praying for deliverance, when a guy in a rowboat comes by. 'Better get in the boat, preacher! The water is rising fast!'
>
> The preacher waves him away. 'No. I have faith in the Lord. He will protect me.' And so, the guy rows away.
>
> The water keeps rising, and the preacher has to retreat to the bell tower. At this point, another guy comes by in a speedboat. 'Get in, preacher! The dam is going to break, and we'll all be washed away!'
>
> Again, the preacher waves him away. 'No. I have faith in the Lord. He will protect me.' And so, the guy guns the engine and zooms away.
>
> The flood waters keep rising, and the preacher is forced to climb to the very top of the steeple. About that time, a police helicopter flies overhead. The cops drop a ladder to the preacher and shout at him: 'Grab the ladder, preacher! The dam has broken, and the water is coming this way fast!'
>
> The preacher waves the chopper away. 'No. I have faith in the Lord. He will protect me.'

Not long after the helicopter flies away, a huge wave of water comes rushing in, and the preacher drowns. He goes to heaven, and he is taken to see God. 'My Lord! I had faith! I prayed to you! Why didn't you save me?!'

And God says, *'What do you want from me? I sent you two boats and a helicopter.'*

Laurie was similar to the man in the parable. She did not listen to the doctor's counsel when they suggested trying medicine. The Spirit was counseling Laurie through His doctors, but Laurie's anxiety stopped her from following through on their advice. It was not until Mary challenged her that she finally gathered the courage to take the prescribed medicine and get the help needed to stop her anxiety. Laurie eventually heard the Holy Spirit's counsel in the Bible verse that Mary found. This verse gave Laurie the courage to try the medication, which, by the grace of God, ended her anxiety.

Mary used the Holy Spirit's gift of fortitude for six years and stuck by Laurie while trying to help her with her anxiety. Mary respected Laurie's need for prayer, but at the same time, tried to motivate Laurie to get further help. She knew that God wanted more for Laurie, so she never gave up.

Even in Laurie's darkest days, she kept her eyes and heart on God. Anxiety may have reduced her to living minute by minute, but she never lost her devotion, or piety, to God. It may even have blinded her early on as she put all her hope in God to relieve her anxiety miraculously. Laurie relied on the Spirit's gift of piety throughout the whole ordeal. Her acceptance of the gift of piety remained strong, and she still models it for her children every day.

Today, Laurie lives her life better able to fear the Lord because she no longer fears her own anxiety. She now has the strength, with new fervor, to accept the Holy Spirit's gift of fearing the Lord. For six long years, Laurie struggled with anxiety. But the Holy Spirit was ever faithful to her. He continually offered her His gifts, kept a friend close, and in the process, brought Laurie even closer to Himself. And we have no doubt that He is doing the same for us.

***
Homework from Heaven
"Advantage Knapsack"/ "Gift Cards"

Materials: "Advantage Knapsack"
- Knapsack (or a small bag that's easy to carry)
- Little Bible
- Small flashlight
- Plastic eyeglasses
- Play cell phone
- Stick of gum
- Small heart-shaped pillow
- Child's compass

What to Do: For Younger Children

Put together a scavenger hunt to help your children create an "advantage" knapsack. Hide objects that will remind your children of the seven gifts of the Holy Spirit. As they find each object, have them put it in their knapsack. Once they've found all the objects, explain how each object represents one of the Gifts of the Holy Spirit. Then, when they explore their world, they will not feel alone because their knapsack will remind them to take advantage of the Holy Spirit's Gifts within them. Here is an example of objects representing each gift of the Spirit:

1. **Wisdom:** A little Bible as a reminder that the Holy Spirit will share His gift of wisdom to help us love better

2. **Understanding:** A small flashlight as a reminder that God lights our way to understand Him better

3. **Knowledge:** Fun plastic glasses as a reminder to always look for more knowledge about our faith

4. **Counsel:** A play cell phone charm as a reminder to "call" on the Holy Spirit for help

5. **Fortitude:** A stick of gum as a reminder to "stick" to a virtuous life

6. **Piety:** A small heart pillow as a reminder to cozy into the love of God while telling Him how much we love, praise, and thank of Him

7. **Fear of the Lord:** A child's compass as a reminder to follow God's ways, not our own

***

Materials: "Gift Cards"
- Index cards
- Sharpies™

What to Do: For Older Children
1. Give seven index cards to each of your children.
2. Have them write one of the gifts of the Spirit on each card.
3. Laminate the cards for lasting power.
4. Each day, week, or month, fan out your children's cards and have them draw one.
5. The gift they select is the gift of the Spirit that they will concentrate on for that day/week/month.
6. Repeat until all the cards have been used or continue it as long as you wish.
7. At supper, have each person share which gift they drew and if they have an example of how that gift helped them that day.

***
Prayerful Pause

Dear Holy Spirit,
Thank You for Your seven gifts.
We accept each and every one.
Amen.

***
Memos to Me

***
Pondering through Pictures

Fruits... Not Just Healthy but Holy

***

"But the wisdom from above is first pure, then peaceable, gentle, willing to yield, full of mercy and good fruits..."
Saint James

Mirror the Spirit's Love

***

To love as the Holy Spirit asks us to means reflecting God's love in our daily lives. What a beautiful goal! When we reflect God's love, we bear the fruit of the Holy Spirit, for we allow the Holy Spirit to live through us. The twelve fruits of the Spirit are modesty, forbearance, chastity, love, joy, peace, patience, kindness, goodness, faithfulness, gentleness, and self-control.

As we strive to mirror the Spirit's love, He smiles. It brings Him that same joy moms experience when we watch our children choose love. So, let us open our hearts to the gift of the Holy Spirit as we begin to discuss His fruits, knowing that they will bring abundant blessings to us and to our households of faith.

The Spirit's Fruits

***

Modesty
Forbearance
Chastity
Love
Joy
Peace
Patience
Kindness
Goodness
Faithfulness
Gentleness
Self-Control

A Modest Approach

***
Mary's Memory
"Holy Boldness"

I remember clearly one afternoon spent with my mother. She worked in the emergency room at the local hospital. We were going there for a quick stop to pick something up in her office. I will never forget that as we entered the hospital, a woman who was yelling approached us. She was wearing a blouse that was unbuttoned down the front. She was very agitated because she thought her ride had forgotten her. I noticed that everyone who walked in ahead of us looked down and walked by quickly. That is precisely what I was prepared to do because I was scared of this woman. I was sixteen and unsure how to handle the situation, so it was easier to ignore it.

Mom, on the other hand, gently walked up to this woman, saying, "It looks like you need help. May I help you?" As she said these words, she began buttoning the woman's blouse. The woman gratefully said, "Oh dear, thank you!" My mom continued, "Are you waiting for someone? Maybe it would help if you sat here where you could see your ride coming." As Mom said this, she got a chair and placed it in the corner, out of the way of people entering the hospital, yet close enough to see out the window toward the pick-up and drop-off area. The woman thanked my mother and sat there calmly. Mom turned to me and said, "Let's go, Mary." As I looked back toward the woman, her ride had pulled in, and someone was helping her to the car. Although Mom never spoke a word to me about the incident, she profoundly affected me that day.

***
Heavenly Hint

"All of you must clothe yourselves with humility in your dealings with one another..."
1 Peter 5:5

***

Reflection

The first fruit of the Spirit we will discuss is modesty. A modest person is unassuming and humble. Recall in Mary's Memory about her mom helping the disheveled woman at the hospital. As an administrator, Mary's mom could have exacerbated the situation by calling for security and making it further uncomfortable for passersby, the woman herself, and ultimately, the people coming to pick her up. But Mary's mom did not do that. She was unassuming in her manner, as she simply took the time to help the woman herself. She quietly and respectfully buttoned her shirt and then found a chair to make her comfortable while waiting for her ride. Mary's mom was modest in her approach to the situation. She did not care about her position as an administrator; rather, she cared for the woman's dignity and then simply moved on with her business. Mary's mom followed the Heavenly Hint by clothing herself in humility and allowing the Spirit to guide her actions. Humility is at the heart of modesty.

Moms, our children deserve the same modest approach that Mary's mom used. There are times when they will find themselves in a predicament and will need our help. We can either help resolve it by making a big scene or take a modest, unassuming approach so as not to embarrass our children. Saint Isaac the Syrian expressed it best when he said, "As salt is needed for all kinds of food, so humility is needed for all kinds of virtues." Here, by virtues, we mean how we approach different situations by choosing to listen to the Spirit in our hearts and acting with humility. Taking the modest approach stands a much better chance of making our children feel loved and cared for just as the woman experienced at the hospital in Mary's memory. So, moms, let us use the Holy Spirit's fruit of modesty in an effort to preserve the dignity of our children in all situations.

***

Homework from Heaven

"Modesty Matters"

Materials:
- Computer or construction paper
- Markers, crayons, colored pencils, paint, stickers
- Glue

What to Do:
1. On the computer paper, write an acrostic using the word "Modesty." For example:

> **M** indful of your behavior
> **O** ver the moon when helping
> **D** ear to each other
> **E** asy to be around
> **S** elfless with your love
> **T** he best version of yourself
> **Y** ieldin' to the Spirit, darlin'
> (We couldn't help ourselves.)

2. Glue the acrostic to the center of the construction paper.
3. Decorate around the word Modesty.

***
Prayerful Pause

Dearest Holy Spirit,
Help us to be unassuming with others
so that they may see You, rather than us,
especially when it comes to
our children's dignity.
Amen.

***
Memos to Me

_____
_____
_____
_____
_____
_____
_____
_____

***
Pondering through Pictures

Strive to Improve

***
Mary's Memory
"Take a Breath"

I have chronic pain in my back and knees due to arthritis. The pain has progressed over the years. I began to recognize that I had become short-tempered because of it. I have to intentionally take a breath before just reacting when my patience is thin due to the pain. And when I do react, I take the time to ask forgiveness in hopes of reconciling any unnecessary hurt I may have caused. Thankfully, I have a forgiving family who sees the best in me, despite myself.

***
Heavenly Hint

"For this reason, I bow my knees before the Father... I pray that, according to the riches of His glory, He may grant that you may be strengthened in your inner being with power through His Spirit..."
Ephesians 3:14,16

***
Reflection

Forbearance is the second fruit of the Spirit. Forbearance allows us to love more fully. It quietly endures wrongs done to us, without provoking the person in turn. The scripture verse in 1 Corinthians 13:7 reminds us, "It (love) bears all things, believes all things, hopes all things, endures all things." As moms, it will help us to remember that sometimes our children get overwhelmed and thus are unintentionally hurtful because of it. On the other hand, sometimes they get under our skin intentionally. We will need daily forbearance to endure these situations calmly and lovingly.

However, there will also be times when our own imperfections get in the way of our vocation. During these times, we especially need to call upon the Holy Spirit's fruit of forbearance to stay faithful to God's calling. Mary's memory above illustrates this. Mary's level of pain can work against her best intentions and when it gets the better of her, she asks for forgiveness.

Forbearance can be difficult, especially when it comes to dealing with our own issues. We all see our own imperfections and try to improve, but some just keep sticking around despite our best efforts. Saint Francis de Sales addressed this issue by saying, "Do not lose courage in considering your own imperfections but instantly set about remedying them - every day begin the task anew." This message is heartening because someone who is striving to be a better person will likely also be a better mom. So, moms, let us take care to use the Spirit's fruit of forbearance to strengthen us in our calling as we strive to improve with each sunrise.

***
Homework from Heaven

"Keep Your Composure"

What to Do:
1. Teach your children not to provoke each other. A little tease now and again is fun, but teasing to the point of frustration is hurtful.
2. Teach your children not to be easily provoked when someone wrongs them. Teach them to take a deep breath or two when someone is aggravating them and not to simply react, thereby not escalating the situation. It's important our children know that they have the power to remain calm and keep their composure.
3. Moms, be aware of how your children provoke you. Don't allow them to take away your ability to keep your composure. You, like your children, have the power to remain calm. Model this, so your children see it, experience it, and can hopefully live it.

***

Prayerful Pause

Dear Holy One,
Please give us the forbearance necessary to work on our imperfections and help our children to work on theirs as well. May we be quick to forgive one another as we go and, therefore, hold on to our joy.
Amen.

✱✱✱
Memos to Me

_____
_____
_____
_____
_____
_____
_____

✱✱✱
Pondering through Pictures

Change of Heart

***

Laurie's Story

"Attitude Adjustment"

After my brother Bob died, my mom and dad had his ashes shipped to Washington State, as Bob had died in New Mexico. When the ashes arrived at the post office, Mom and Dad went to get them. The person helping them at the counter was short with them. Once the person went back to retrieve their package, he realized what they were picking up, as the box had the word "deceased" on it. When he returned, his attitude was much different. He was very pleasant and patient.

***

Heavenly Hint

"Create in me a clean heart, O God, and put a new and right spirit within me."
Psalm 51

***

Reflection

The third fruit of the Spirit is chastity. To be chaste is to be pure of heart. We've talked about how our thoughts affect our behavior. Now, we want to talk about how the condition of a person's heart affects their attitude.

[10]There is a movie where the coaches of a boys' football team talk about just this. "What's your attitude like?" one of the coaches asks a player. This particular player had a bad attitude. The coach continues, "Your attitude is a reflection of your heart. If your heart is not right with God, your attitude will follow. If your attitude stinks, your heart is not in the right place." If we have an "attitude," we are hard-pressed to love with a pure heart as the Holy Spirit calls us to.

As in Laurie's Story above, we all have bad days that can cause angst in our hearts and incite bad attitudes. The man who helped Laurie's Mom and Dad did not have a good attitude when they first came to him. However, when he realized what they were there for, he had a change of heart and adjusted his attitude.

Moms, when we experience angst in our hearts from the occasional overwhelming pressures of being a mom, we suggest turning to the Holy Spirit's love within us and accepting His guidance to allow a change of heart in us. We can always count on Him to help us in such times, whether through prayer, meditation, spiritual readings, scripture, or by allowing ourselves to have a good cry. A good cry can help us release some of that angst and help our hearts to feel lighter. Saint Pope John Paul II said, "It's better to cry than be angry, because anger hurts others while tears flow silently through the soul and cleanse the heart." Moms, let us be good to ourselves and others by allowing ourselves to cry from time to time. We cannot always be on top of our game.

***
Homework from Heaven
"Cleansing the Heart"

What to Do:
Give your children and yourself permission to cry. Teach your children that crying is not a sign of weakness, quite the opposite. It is a sign of strength because we are acknowledging our need for God. For again, as Saint Pope John Paul II said, "Tears flow silently through the soul to cleanse our heart." Crying is an emotional reset. Once the tears stop flowing, there is a sense of peace that fills the heart. Our tears help "create a clean heart and put a new and right Spirit within us," as the scripture said in the Heavenly Hint. Our tears might not change the situation, but they definitely change our hearts.

***
Prayerful Pause

Spirit of Love,
Help us to deal with the angst in our
hearts by finding Your love within us.
Keep us from hurting others or ourselves
by allowing You to change our hearts.
Amen.

***
Memos to Me

_____
_____
_____
_____
_____
_____
_____

***
Pondering through Pictures

Generous Love

***

Mary's Memory
"Listening Attentively"

One day, I saw my son, Patrick, walk into the room and begin talking to his dad. His dad was neither facing him, nor looking at him as he was focused on his tablet. As Patrick talked, he leaned around his dad, trying to catch his eyes. Aaron was not yet ready to give Patrick his full attention but had not indicated this to him. While watching the two of them, it came to me that there are times when stopping everything, looking at our children, and attentively listening is what they need. If Aaron had turned and looked at Patrick, he would have immediately known this because it was written all over his son's face. In that moment what Patrick was saying was important to him, and he needed his dad to look at him, so He felt truly heard.

***

Heavenly Hint

*"Each one should give
as much as he has decided
on his own initiative, not reluctantly
or under compulsion, for God
loves a cheerful giver."*
2 Corinthians 9:7

***

Reflection

We have now come to the Fruits of the Spirit, and the first is love. We have already discussed love in several ways throughout the book. However, when exploring it as one of the Holy Spirit's fruits, we will discuss generous love. There are a million ways to be generous with love, from giving a cup of sugar to a neighbor to adjusting our entire lives to care for a loved one in need. But what if we discussed generosity of love in terms of our attention? Philippians affirms this idea "Let each of you look not to your own interests, but to the interests of others."

How often do we generously and cheerfully give our love through undivided attention to those around us? Being generous with our undivided attention means honestly giving ourselves to the other person, despite the sacrifice, and asking nothing in return. This is generous love. It imitates God because He is always there for us and gives us His undivided attention.

Giving our undivided attention to our family is vital. Unfortunately, we are all occasionally guilty of the simple example in Mary's Memory. We know this because we have lived it. We well know that moms cannot just stop what they are doing every time their children need to talk. That is why it is easy to say things like, "Talk to me while I'm cooking supper." Perhaps, though, it is better to pause and tell our children that we cannot give them our full attention right now but are willing to listen. Ask if they need our undivided attention for this conversation, and if they do, tell them that we would be happy to give it to them after supper. It is a simple thing, but sometimes, that is what our children need.

Whenever possible, consider stopping everything, dropping everything - that is special, especially when done with a cheerful heart. Dropping everything, looking someone in the eye, and focusing solely on them is a simple concept, often brushed over but worthy of our consideration. That tells the other person that we so love them, that they are worthy of our time.

These are the moments that stick with people because, as

the Christmas song [11]"O Holy Night" says, "The soul feels it's worth." All people, including our children, need to feel their worth. So says Saint John Bosco, "It's not enough to love, people have to feel that they are loved." So, moms, let us be generous with our love by being generous with our attention. Love is a Fruit of the Spirit and giving it generously with our undivided attention allows the Holy Spirit to live through us.

***

Homework from Heaven

"Letters of Love"

What to Do:

Mary has another way that she gives generous love with her undivided attention. From time to time throughout her children's lives, she writes them a letter of love. It is random and for no particular reason. The letter is always encouraging and hopefully inspiring, as she expresses what she thinks her children need to hear at that time in their lives. Occasionally, Mary will include a little gift that she knows her children will like. For example, she once added superhero Pez™ candy because her children were into them that summer. Once she finishes the letter, which always includes stickers, Mary's known for those, she places the letter in an envelope and then places it on her children's pillows, so they will find it before they go to bed. This way, they fall asleep with their mom's loving thoughts in their minds and hearts. We suggest you try this too. Your children will love it!

***
Prayerful Pause

*Spirit of Love,
Please help us to give our love generously, especially when it comes to our undivided attention. May our children feel deeply loved, as we choose to spend time focusing our attention on them.
Amen.*

***
Memos to Me

_____
_____
_____
_____
_____
_____
_____

***
Pondering through Pictures

A Spirit of Joy

***

Mary's Memory

"Suppertime"

My mom and dad placed a high priority on eating supper around the table. They believed that when a family sits at the table to share a meal, it brings them closer together. Every evening, we waited to eat until everyone got home from their activities, whether it be football or volleyball practice or an after-school job. Suppers were late at the Chilton household. We'd sit and listen to each other's stories and support one another's endeavors.

My dad did silly things that made supper fun. For instance, few of us liked peas, so he would take his knife and slide it under the pile of peas on his plate then slowly raise it as high as his glass. The amount of peas he got on his knife was the amount we had to eat. Shaking the table gently or doing something to startle him was allowed. Some suppers we got lucky, others Dad did, but we almost always got a laugh. If I remember correctly, my dad's record was fourteen peas. The point is that we tried to make suppertime a time of joy throughout the ups and downs of our family life. Mom's and Dad's priority to create family time around the table was so life-giving that all of my siblings and I have carried that family tradition into our own homes.

***
Heavenly Hint

*"I (Jesus) have told you this so that
My own joy may be in you and your joy
may be complete."*
John 15:11

***
Reflection

Joy is the second fruit of the Spirit. Saint Bonaventure says, "A spiritual joy is the greatest sign of the Divine grace dwelling in a soul." Joy is rooted in God and comes from the Holy Spirit. Saint Teresa of Calcutta tells us that "Joy is a net of love by which we catch souls." Moms, for our children's souls, hearts, and minds to desire God, it will have to bring them joy, and that starts with our approach to life in the faith.

Moms, our family's faith life should be rooted in the Holy Spirit's fruit of joy. For joy comes from the Spirit. The world tells us to seek happiness. But happiness is fleeting. Happiness comes from what is happening in our lives at the present time. When things are going well, we are happy. However, when sorrow strikes, our happiness leaves us. Joy never leaves us. It is a part of us because the Holy Spirit is in us. Once when struggling with the death of someone Mary loved dearly, her friend wrote Mary a letter. In it, she quoted Robert Schuller saying, "Mary, 'joy is not the absence of suffering. It is the presence of God.'" This truth never left Mary, and it helped to hold her together during that difficult time and others. It helped Mary to cling to the Spirit and find His joy in her.

So how do we rely on the Spirit's joy? One way is to establish family traditions that intentionally bring God's complete joy to the family. Our families need traditions to celebrate our faith. Traditions tug at our heartstrings. They create memories that bring the family closer to each other and closer to God. We hold traditions in our hearts. They stir the love and joy that comes with them as in Mary's Memory above. To this day, she can still see her family sitting around the table, the same table that sits in her dining room today, and that her family enjoys meals around each night. It brings her comfort and joy.

We can always be joyful people despite our circumstances because joy is not the absence of suffering, it is the presence of God. Let us bring the presence of God to our families whenever we can. How do we do this? We do what Saint Paul told the people in Philippians 2:1-2, "So if in Christ there is anything that will move you, any incentive in love, any fellowship in the Spirit, any warmth or sympathy - I appeal to you, make my joy complete by being of a single mind, one in love, one in heart and one in mind." Mothers, we need to encourage our families to live what Paul describes in this scripture. We can bring Jesus' presence into our households of faith by being of a single mind, one in love, one in heart, and one in mind. Paul said that his joy would be made complete when he saw the people of Philippi doing this. Moms, may we too experience complete joy as we watch our family participate in our traditions as we together bring the presence of God into our household of faith.

***

Homework from Heaven

"Faith Traditions"

What to Do:

This year, establish some new faith traditions. Try to think of ideas that will help to keep your family in a joyful and holy frame of mind. Here are a couple of ideas:

1. Mary has a faith tradition that is tied to her Christmas Eve birthday. On Christmas Eve, Mary had her birthday supper,

gifts and cake, between three and four in the afternoon. Once the celebration was over, so was Mary's birthday. Her family would then turn their attention to getting ready for Christmas Mass at seven. Upon returning home from church, each child got to open two presents and Aaron got to open one (Mary already had her fair share of presents). The first present was a pair of Christmas pajamas and that's what Aaron got to open with the children. The second present was for the children alone and was from Aaron and Mary. It was an ornament that represented something that they liked from that year or something that they accomplished. After reminiscing about why Patrick, Kathleen, and Maggie got the ornaments they did, the children would hang them on the tree. Then, they would all scurry away to put on their pajamas and Aaron would tuck them into bed, telling them "The sooner you get to sleep, the sooner morning will come." Mary and Aaron intentionally had this tradition in order to distinguish Mary's birthday from our Savior's birthday. Once Mass began, so did the celebration of Jesus' birth. Consider getting ready to celebrate Christmas with your family by starting this pajama and an ornament tradition with your family. You don't have to have a Christmas Eve birthday for the magic of Christmas to begin this way. It makes for a tree full of memories for your children when they move into their own homes and have their own tree.
2. Celebrate the New Year with a house blessing on the feast of Epiphany, January 6th, by using holy water to bless each room of your house. Start with a prayer asking God to bless and protect your home. Then walk around your house sprinkling each room with holy water. Let a different member of the family bless each room. Then, celebrate with your family's favorite dessert.
3. Now, it's your turn! Be creative. Ask people what they do for their family faith traditions. Look on the internet for ideas. Choose traditions that you know your family will delight in.

***
Prayerful Pause

*Holy Spirit,
May we always seek Your presence in our
lives for You are our joy.
Amen.*

***
Memos to Me

***
Pondering through Pictures

Peace Prevails

***

Laurie's Story
"Gift of God"

It had been five and a half years since Steve and I had had our seventh child, Sarah Joy. At that point, we thought that our family was complete: one boy and six girls. It felt right because both Steve and I had come from families that each had seven children. Around this time, I found out that I was pregnant. I was really shocked and began to feel overwhelmed. When I told Steve the news, he also began to feel overwhelmed.

One day, early in my pregnancy, I had a panic attack. "Oh no," I thought, "Here we go again - the pregnancy is starting to take its toll on me already. If I start to have panic attacks this early in the pregnancy, I'm in trouble. How will I get through eight more months of panic?" Also, when I went in for my initial O.B. appointment, they had to draw my blood. The technician filled up one vial, then two, three, four vials. At this point, I was wondering how much longer this would take. As she began filling the fifth vial, I didn't feel very well. I started feeling faint and asked for a glass of water. The technician responded by making sure I got some. I drank it then put my head down on my legs and asked for a cold cloth. I was scared and I remember asking Mother Mary to help me through this. The cold water and cloth were helping me, as the technician finished the fifth vial. Thankfully, that was the last one, and I slowly began to feel better. "Oh boy, not only am I going to have problems with panic, but I don't seem to be able to handle even a blood draw, which I normally don't have problems with." I continued feeling overwhelmed.

Part of my concern was that with each pregnancy, the new hormones threw off my body chemistry, and would require the doctor to adjust my anxiety medications. No two pregnancies were alike. It was a bit of a guessing game. Given my past experiences, I wasn't looking forward to an uptick in my anxiety as the doctor and I figured out my meds. But to my surprise and abundant relief, God answered my prayers. I didn't have to change a thing.

One day, after I dropped the kids off at school, I stopped by the church to pray. It was early in my first trimester, and I started crying. The question came to mind whether or not having another child was God's will for our family. Steve and I had always been open to life. After seven children, that was still the case, but since we hadn't gotten pregnant for five and a half years, we weren't expecting to get pregnant again.

The day finally came when I thought I was going into labor. Steve and I went over to the hospital and sure enough, I was dilated to an eight. Wow, an eight! I quickly asked and got an epidural, and as many times happened with epidurals, my labor slowed down. At this point, the nurse left the room. Labor continued and just a few short hours later, my doctor was telling me to push. We never found out the gender of our babies ahead of time, so we had no clue if it was a boy or a girl. I was so excited to find out and as the baby was born, I asked Steve, "What is it, what is it!?"

"It's a boy!"

"A boy!" A rush of joy filled my heart! Our oldest son Sam was seventeen years old now and he had never gotten a little brother. In fact, when I first told Sam that we were expecting baby number eight, he was not very happy. He probably figured it would be yet another girl to further outnumber him. However, when he found out he had a baby brother, he was thrilled, and said, "It's about time." Now, our family is bookended by two boys, with six girls in between. It was perfect!

As the nurse placed our newborn in my arms, Steve and I realized that we had not considered names yet and that we had better get on it. So, Steve went out to the nurse's station and came back with a book of names. He opened the book and said, "What do you think of the name Jonathan?"

"Jonathan...hmm... What does the name Jonathan mean?"

"It means 'Gift of God,'" "Yes, I love that. We'll name him Jonathan Robert, Robert in honor of my dad." My heart was at peace as I knew Jonathan was a precious gift to our family. I had caused myself undue anxiety. I should've trusted in God's plan all along. Our sweet baby, Jonathan Robert, became the apple of nine people's eyes.

***

Heavenly Hint

"Peace, I bequeath to you, my own peace, I give you, a peace which the world cannot give, this is my gift to you. Do not let your hearts be troubled or afraid."
John 14:27

***

Reflection

The third fruit of the Spirit we will discuss is peace. All mothers have struggles within themselves that can cause them to lose their peace. Like Laurie in her story above, when she lost her peace as she struggled to determine if getting pregnant was God's will. When Laurie heard the meaning of Jonathan's name and gazed into his eyes, she realized her question was silly. Rather than worrying, Laurie could have sought the Spirit of peace in her life and discovered that her pregnancy was, of course, God's plan all along. Psalm 127:3 shows this truth perfectly, "Sons are a birthright from Yahweh, children are a reward from Him." Jonathan was indeed a precious gift given to her family by God, a soul to love for all eternity.

When life happens and unexpected events drain us of our peace, we moms often move to auto-pilot. Once on autopilot, we are not at our best. Our responses can be hurtful either to others or to ourselves. They are habits we have developed over time and some we may not even like. This happened in Laurie's story above. When Laurie found herself pregnant, she was scared and felt out of control. Rather than turning to the Spirit of peace, she fell into old habits and allowed anxiety to take hold.

How do we change habitual responses? We turn to the Holy Spirit for help. "Who except God can give us peace?" asked Saint Gerard Majella. However, breaking unwanted habits is not always easy. In fact, often, it is tough. Each time that dreaded habit resurfaces, we recognize it, and we can make a different choice. Breaking an unwanted habit will take intention, practice, and patience with ourselves, but the Spirit will never fail, and peace will prevail.

***

Homework from Heaven

"Finding Peace"

Materials:
- A smooth stone
- Sharpies™
- "The Prayer of Saint Francis" in number six of this "What to Do."

What to Do:
1. Go outside and find a smooth stone that fits easily in the palm of your hand. Give yourself about fifteen minutes to sit in a quiet place alone.
2. Roll the stone around gently in your hands, asking the Spirit to help you discern which habitual responses to let go of, along with the negative emotions that come with them.
3. Keep rolling the stone, allowing it to become the responses and emotions. If it would help you, write words on the

stone that name these responses.
4. When you feel as if you cannot stand holding that stone for even one more second because it is heavy with all the feelings that go along with the responses, put it in a bag so you don't have to see it.
5. Then, go to a safe spot where you can throw the stone into a body of water, such as a lake, river, bay, or the ocean. Then turn and leave it all behind.
6. Next, find a peaceful place to reflect on "The Prayer of Saint Francis" written below. [12]If you'd prefer listening to it in a song, refer to the footnote at the bottom of this page. This website will lead you to hear Angelina Davis sing this prayer as she walks through Saint Francis' hometown of Assisi, Italy. Below, we have written the song as Angelina sings it in case you want to read while listening or sing along. Listening to it or singing it is our favorite way to pray "The Prayer of Saint Francis," who's song title is "Make Me a Channel of Your Peace."

"Make Me a Channel of Your Peace"
(The Prayer of Saint Francis)

"Make me a channel of Your peace
where there is hatred, let me bring Your love
where there is injury, Your pardon Lord
and where there's doubt, true faith in You.
Make me a channel of Your peace
where there's despair in life, let me bring hope
where there is darkness, only light
and where there's sadness, ever joy.
Oh Master, grant that I may never seek
so much to be consoled as to console
to be understood as to understand

to be loved as to love with all my soul.
Make me a channel of Your peace
it is pardoning that we are pardoned
in giving of ourselves that we receive
and in dying that we're born to eternal life.
Oh Master, grant that I may never seek
so much to be consoled as to console
to be understood as to understand
and to love as to love with all my soul.
Make me a channel of Your peace
it is pardoning that we are pardoned
in giving of ourselves that we receive
and in dying that we're born to eternal life.
Make me a channel of Your peace."

This simple activity can transform a person because it allows us to let go of a habit we never wanted, by allowing the Holy Spirit to change us.

***

Prayerful Pause

Dear Spirit,
Thank You for Your sweet fruit of peace.
Please help me to live in such a way that I
may be at peace within myself and also be
a channel of Your peace to others.
Amen.

***
Memos to Me

***
Pondering through Pictures

Waiting with Grace

***
Mary's Memory
"Waiting Patiently"

Once when I was at Laurie's house, Laurie had to run an errand. I stayed back as Rose and Hannah had asked me to play the word game Rummikub™. Hannah invited Steve into the game, so they decided to play in teams. It was Steve and Hannah versus Rose and me. Rummikub™ is so named because its tiles are used to form runs and sets like in the card game Rummy. There are four sets of tiles. Each set is numbered one through twelve and has its own color. The game begins with each team randomly picking up fourteen tiles. These tiles are the equivalent of a hand in Rummy. The game's objective is to be the first player to empty their rack of tiles by forming them into runs and sets and placing them down on the table. A player can take tiles from the opponent's side of the table and use them to form runs or sets, as long as there is at least one tile from the player's own rack to lay down. If they cannot, they must return the opponent's tiles, and forfeit their turn.

Rose and I were thick into the game and took some of Steve and Hannah's tiles, using as many of our own as possible to make new runs and sets. While Rose and I were busily moving tiles about, Steve offhandedly commented that he didn't understand why we needed to physically move the tiles to create new combinations. Rose said we were trying to make new runs and sets with the tiles. Steve nodded and patiently waited while Rose and I continued trying to make our combinations work. We had no luck, so we forfeited our turn.

Once we gave up, Steve remarked that once he had seen the new tiles that we had taken from our rack, he knew that there were no combinations. I asked, "You mean you don't have to move the tiles around?" Steve answered, "No, I can just see in my head what works and what doesn't." I was astounded because there was no way I could just see it in my head. I have to physically move the tiles. It was then that it struck me that everyone who plays this game does not have to go to such efforts to move each tile around to make the combinations and that they wait to let me. Steve and Hannah sat there patiently waiting for Rose and me to make ours move even though they saw that it wouldn't work from the get-go. Steve and Hannah happily gave us the time we needed.

***

Heavenly Hint

*"Lead a life worthy
of the vocation
to which you were called.
With all humility and gentleness,
and with patience, support
each other in love."
Ephesians 4:1-2*

***

Reflection

The fourth fruit of the Spirit is patience. One definition of patience is to wait without getting angry; we simply wait with grace. God created people to be different from one another. What comes easily to one person may be difficult for another. We all think differently. We learn and grow at our own pace. For this reason, we should follow the Heavenly Hint above by being patient and supporting each other in love. Moms, we will need to be patient, not because things are going wrong, but rather to let our children become who they are meant to be in their own time.

Patience allows people to be who they are. Patience loves people enough to give them the time they need to achieve what they are trying to do. This is what happened above when Steve and Hannah loved Rose and Mary enough to give them the time they needed to take their turns. Even though it may seem like a small thing, it is not. The Spirit's fruit of patience allows people to shine in both their efforts and their accomplishments.

Moms, our children are individuals who will develop at their own pace. Saint Francis de Sales told us, "Have patience to walk with short steps until you have wings to fly." There will be many short steps in the course of our children's lifetime. Our job is to walk beside them patiently, not rushing or judging them, and especially not comparing them to others. None of our children are exactly alike. Our children will grow their wings at their own pace. One may fly early, another later, but that's okay. God has His plans and His timing for each of our children. [13]Mother Angelica, the founder of the Eternal Word Television Network (EWTN), once said, "Patience is adjusting your time to God's time." Moms, we are our children's support system. We need to be patient with them throughout our vocation of motherhood, and we need to teach our children to be patient with themselves. As we adjust to God's timing, may we live out the remarkable love that the Holy Spirit calls us to through patience with everyone around us, especially those in our family.

***

Homework from Heaven

"Please Be Patient"

What to Do:
1. Sit down with your children and ask them, "Where are there times in your life when you wish I would be more patient with you? Be honest, I love you and I want to be more patient with you when you need it."
2. Now ask them, "Are there times when you can be more

patient with your siblings, or with me?" How do you think patience would change the situation?
3. Remind our children that we all change, learn, and grow at our own pace, and being patient with each other will give us the grace to do just that.

***

Prayerful Pause

*Dear Holy Spirit,
Help us to foster patience
in our households of faith, thus allowing
each member of our family, the time to
grow and bloom at their own pace.
Amen.*

***
Memos to Me

_____
_____
_____
_____
_____
_____
_____
_____

***
Pondering through Pictures

Cultivating Kind People

***

Laurie's Story
"Walking in the Road"

One day when driving home after picking my kids up from school, I noticed an elderly woman walking in the road carrying groceries. Since there was only gravel on both sides of the road, and the woman was using a walker, it forced her to walk out on the road. People driving past this woman were clearly annoyed because they had to slow down to go around her and showed their irritation as they drove by. When I got closer, I realized that there was no need for irritation because this elderly woman just needed help. So, I slowly pulled up beside her and offered to take her where she needed to go. She accepted and we were on our way.

***

Heavenly Hint

"Set your minds on things that are above not on things that are on earth..."
Colossians 3:2

***

Reflection

Kindness is the fifth fruit of the Spirit. There are many types of kindness. We want to emphasize a particular kindness not spoken about enough - kindness in our thoughts. Genuine kindness stems first from love, Scripture tells us in Romans 8:5, "For those who live according to the flesh set their minds on the things of the flesh, but those who live according to the Spirit set their minds on the things of the Spirit." In Laurie's Story, the other drivers' minds were not in a place of kindness, and their actions demonstrated it. Laurie, however, followed the Scripture above that day. She kept her mind, or thoughts, on what the Spirit desired. Keeping kind thoughts helps us to do what the Spirit desires because it encourages us to think about the other person and what they may be going through. Hence, we are more likely to respond in such a way that the other person knows we care. Scripture tells us in Proverbs 31:26, "She opens her mouth with wisdom, and the teaching of kindness is on her tongue." To imitate God's kindness, we should never let kindness leave us, for thinking kind thoughts drives doing kind deeds.

Moms, we can make kind thoughts a habit. Since it is well advised to start a good habit young, let us teach our children to think kind thoughts too. After all, kind thoughts create kind hearts and kind hearts create kind people. Saint Basil tells us, "He who plants kindness gathers love." As we plant kind thoughts in our minds, our actions will reflect God's love for others.

When her children were young, Laurie helped teach this concept using a song that speaks to the importance of our thoughts. Unfortunately, the author is unknown, but the title of the song is, [14]"Oh Be Careful Little Eyes." Part of the lyric says, "Be careful little mind what you think, be careful little mind what you think, for the Father up above is looking down in love, oh be careful little mind what you think." This song teaches our children to be careful about their thoughts. It does not mean to do it out of fear but out of love. The Father up above is looking down with love and wants us to keep our thoughts on His love and feel and share that same love. Remember, kind thoughts help create kind hearts and kind hearts create kind people.

So, mothers, let us allow kindness to permeate our minds and teach our children to do the same. Let us use the Holy Spirit's fruit of kindness to inspire us to keep our minds set on the Spirit and, therefore, do what He desires.

***

Homework from Heaven

"Letter to Self" / "Turn It Around"

Materials: "Letter to Self"
- Pens
- Paper
- Envelopes

What to Do:

This activity is to encourage your children to fill their minds with kind thoughts about themselves. When they are young and optimistic, have your children sit down and write a letter telling all of the things they like about themselves and what they like to do. Put the letter in an envelope and save it. When your children hit adolescence and if they start losing confidence or develop insecurities, get out the letter and read it to them. Remind them that they are that same wonderful person with those same qualities and gifts.

***

What to Do: "Turn It Around"

1. Remind your children to be kind to themselves by maintaining kind thoughts about themselves. Start this young, for it will be easier for them to make a good habit out of it. Emphasize how important it is to have positive self-talk. Maintaining a positive outlook about yourself will allow you to be more kind to people around you as well.
2. When you hear your children say something like, "My drawing isn't good. I'll never be an artist," help them to turn that thought around into something more positive, such as, "My drawing may not be what I pictured in my mind, but I am still learning. I will get better."

3. Remind your children to think and speak kind truths about themselves. Have them practice it. You can even go as far as to have them look at themselves in the mirror and tell themselves they are beautiful and name things they like about themselves. Being kind to ourselves is important because people who love themselves are more able to love others. As the Lord said in Matthew 22:39, "You shall love your neighbor as yourself." If you can't love yourself, then how are you supposed to love your neighbor? Kind thoughts create kind people and kind thoughts start with you.

***

Prayerful Pause

*Dear Spirit,
Please help us to make a habit
of thinking kind thoughts and
encouraging our children to
think kind thoughts
about themselves.
Amen.*

✽✽✽
Memos to Me

✽✽✽
Pondering through Pictures

Overcoming Self-Doubt

***

Mary's Memory

"You Have What It Takes"

Throughout my life, teachers told my parents and me that I wasn't smart enough to succeed. Many of them used the word retarded to describe me. (I am so sorry if that word has offended you. It offends me horribly. Sadly, teachers used this word in my youth.) As an adult, it was determined I had ADD, but back then, they'd never heard of ADD. This, in part, explains why I had difficulty in school and why my teachers would think this of me. Not only did I struggle in school, but I never passed a standardized test because the time restraint paralyzed me. My mind would go blank, and I couldn't even remember many of the questions long enough to answer them. So, I ended up guessing. I felt like a failure. The combination of all of this, coupled with my not being a confident child, created a lot of self-doubt in me. Self-doubt would continue to rear its ugly head after I had been accepted into a Catholic preparatory high school because after being accepted, I was once again told I was not smart enough to succeed. This dashed my hopes of going to high school with my closest friends and continuing to learn about God.

The spring before entering high school, my friends and I took the high school's entrance exam. Several weeks after the test, I was asked to return and write an essay explaining why I wanted to attend the school. My friends and I anxiously waited to hear the results. Sometime early that summer, we all got our acceptance letters. I was surprised and elated because I didn't expect to pass, as I never had before. My friends and I were so happy and also anxious about the unknown. But we knew that we would be okay because we'd still be together.

***

Heavenly Hint

"We know that all things work together for good for those who love God, who are called according to His purpose."
Romans 8:28

***

Reflection

Goodness is the sixth fruit of the Spirit. It is in God's goodness that He places holy desires and hopes in our hearts. We know that these desires and hopes come from God when their fulfillment brings His goodness into our lives and the lives of others. God would not place empty desires and hopes into our hearts. Our children must know this. As Saint Thérèse of Lisieux put it, "To limit your desires and your hopes is to misunderstand God's infinite goodness!"

Mothers, it is very important to share the same enthusiastic goodness that God has for His children with our children. However, all too often, self-doubt rears its ugly head. Self-doubt can put limitations on our children. If we allow our children to doubt themselves, it could mean they are doubting God. Doubting God stifles our children's ability to spread His goodness into the world. We can clarify that our hopes and desires have come from God by taking the time to pray and discern about them.

Prayer and discernment are important to teach our children. When they determine that their desire or hope truly came from God, it can give them the confidence to act on those desires and hopes, rather than let self-doubt stifle them. Our children can move forward with what God has placed in their hearts and, therefore, spread His goodness.

In Mary's Memory above, self-doubt plagued Mary. Her

counselor had told her that she would not succeed in school. While it was not without its struggles, Mary stuck to it and went on to graduate from college. Mary's mom and dad never let her self-doubt get the best of her. Despite teachers telling her the contrary, Mary's parents constantly reminded her of the truth, that the teachers and the counselor were wrong, and that she had what it took to achieve her dream of going to high school with her friends and continuing to learn about God. From the beginning, Mary's parents perpetually encouraged her to believe in herself. They told her she was smart and could do anything she put her mind to. In hindsight, Mary recognizes God's goodness in her parents for their unwavering belief in her.

It is easy for our children to lose sight of the big picture during times of self-doubt. Moms, we can help our children see that vision again. So, do not let self-doubt limit your children. Instead, teach them to trust in the goodness of God, knowing that He has already given them what they need to achieve the desires and hopes that He has placed in their hearts.

***

Homework from Heaven

"Open Their Eyes"

What to Do:
1. When the world tries to blind our children with self-doubt, moms must consistently open our children's eyes to the truth and not let them give up on themselves, or the dreams that the Spirit placed in their hearts.
2. As Mary's parents did for her, it is our job to help our children share God's goodness. We do this by advocating and encouraging our children to pursue the desires and hopes God placed in them and support them in that pursuit. This will take prayer, conversations, and at times, doing it beside them until they can do it for themselves. Ask for the Holy Spirit's gifts of wisdom, understanding, and counsel

to guide you and your child in this process.

***

Prayerful Pause

*Dear Holy Spirit,
Please help our children to hold tight to the hopes and desires that You placed in their hearts and not let them be overcome by self-doubt.
Amen*

✱✱✱
Memos to Me

✱✱✱
Pondering through Pictures

Ever Faithful

***

Laurie's Story

"The List Goes On and On"

I'll never forget the day the doctor told me that my daughter, Sarah, had Hodgkin's Lymphoma. At that moment, my world turned upside down. My twelve-year-old girl had cancer.

Life instantly sped up as the clinic staff scheduled us for multiple appointments over the course of the next three days. My husband, Steve, told his three sisters the situation and they made a dinner a day to help feed our troops. We so appreciated their thoughtfulness and quick response.

During those appointments, we met with an entire team of doctors, nurses, and other staff who would all play a role in helping us navigate Sarah's cancer treatment. Sarah's doctor was confident that he had the knowledge and resources necessary for Sarah to have a good outcome. It felt good knowing we were in capable hands.

Sarah's school soon heard the news. Teachers and staff were overwhelmed with a desire to help and put together thoughtful gifts, cards, and even money. We were blown away. Sarah's classmates made cards for her with heartfelt messages and prayers. As if what the school community did wasn't enough, Sarah's soccer team had a fundraiser to help pay for Sarah's medical expenses.

Once treatment got underway, Sarah's sister Beth supported her by going to every appointment and surgery. Sarah's other sister Amy came to everything that she possibly could. Sarah found extra joy during the times when Amy was able to bring her baby girl, Alyssa. Alyssa was a good distraction. When Sarah had to stay overnight at the hospital for multiple days in a row, her best friend bought her a pretty pair of pajamas and a soft blanket. Family and friends, including Mary and her girls, came to visit Sarah. All of the love and support brought comfort to a situation that could have been scary and lonely. Sarah felt the love.

Chemotherapy did its dreadful thing, as it often does, and Sarah's hair began falling out. One of Steve's patients, who specializes in fitting wigs for cancer patients, offered to work with Sarah to help her get the most natural-looking wig available. I took Sarah to meet with him for the various fittings. He was so kind and treated Sarah with such gentleness and respect. He was positive and encouraging and made Sarah feel comfortable. Once we had chosen and ordered the wig, Steve's staff graciously paid for it.

The list goes on and on. We know that many people were praying for Sarah and those prayers were powerful. For instance, Sarah's energy level never waned during her fight against cancer. She continued playing soccer, and her labs consistently showed no negative effects from the chemo. The grace from those prayers sustained Sarah. After completing chemo, Sarah was rechecked and given a clean bill of health.

During this trial, everyone's generosity and kindness were overwhelming, and we were grateful. God's faithfulness was also overwhelming as He took care of Sarah throughout her struggle with cancer. He was there for her when she needed Him most.

***

Heavenly Hint

"Yahweh Himself will lead you; He will be with you; He will not fail you or desert you. Have no fear, do not be alarmed."
Deuteronomy 31:8

***
Reflection

The seventh fruit of the Spirit is faithfulness. When we think about God's faithfulness, we know we can always count on God being God. His character does not change. He is always trustworthy and reliable. Faithfulness has the word faith in it for a purpose. Our faith in God reminds us to be like Him, trustworthy and reliable. There is comfort in knowing we can count on those we need. Psalm 46:1-2 says, "God is both refuge and strength for us, a help always ready in trouble; so, we shall not be afraid…"

Being a mom is not for the faint of heart. There are times when it may feel as if our worlds are falling apart around us. It is at these times when we must hold fast to God's faithfulness, knowing that He is trustworthy and that we can rely on Him to help us through the storms of motherhood. God is faithful to all His children. The Spirit moves with love through our lives and inspires people to help each other. For Laurie, He was faithful by giving Sarah people that she could count on to help her through the storm. God was ever-present in Sarah's time of trouble by providing what she needed.

Another point about faithfulness stems from a quote by Saint Teresa of Calcutta: "God has not called me to be successful. He has called me to be faithful." We may not always feel successful in everything we do as mothers. But that is okay because God is not looking for us to be successful in our own eyes or in the world's measure of success. The Spirit desires our faithfulness to Him, just as He is faithful to us. God does not expect us to do everything perfectly or to attain every goal we set for ourselves. He does not grade us. Rather, He calls us to rely on Him, to stay faithful to Him, just as He is ever faithful to us.

***
Homework from Heaven

"Prayer Chain"

Materials:
- Computer paper
- Scissors
- Stapler
- Markers or pens with enough colors for each family member
- Three-wick candle: one wick for the Father, one for the Son, and one for the Holy Spirit
- Matches

What to Do:

How many times has someone asked you to pray about something, and you happily agree? You want to and then it slips your mind. Here is a way to help your family remember those prayer requests.

1. Create a box, bin, or basket to hold all the materials. Keep it in a handy place, readily available to all family members.
2. Cut the computer paper into 2"x11" strips. Have each family member choose a color of marker or pen that only they will use to write their prayer requests. Keep the strips, markers, and stapler in the basket ready to go.
3. As the prayer requests come in, write each one down on a strip of paper. Moms, ask your little ones what they would like to pray for, so they can participate.
4. Keep in mind that not all prayer requests will be the same length. If writing a request uses up just a little bit of a strip, put more than one on it. But if you need the whole strip for one request, then use it. Have each family member link their own strips together to form a small chain.

5. These individual small chains will eventually link together to create one long family prayer chain to remind you to pray for those requests made by family members and friends.
6. Make time to pray for these requests weekly, bi-weekly, monthly, or whatever works for your family. To start, light the candle. Have everyone sit around the table and have each person take turns praying out loud for their prayer requests on their individual chain. Then, have them link their small chain to the next person's small chain by stapling it. The next person then prays their prayer requests out loud, and links their chain to the next person's chain, until everyone's chains are linked together.
7. Remember to look at past prayer requests and remove the answered ones. As you remove them, thank the Spirit for His faithfulness.

***

Prayerful Pause

Dear Faithful Spirit,
We thank You for always being there for us through thick and thin. Help us to always strive to be faithful to You within our households of faith.
Amen.

***
Memos to Me

_____
_____
_____
_____
_____
_____
_____
_____

***
Pondering through Pictures

Avoid Insult to Injury

***

Mary's Memory

"Boom"

When my husband, Aaron was in his early twenties, he had worked hard to make enough money to buy a truck outright. He was proud of himself and happy with his new truck. Shortly after purchasing it, he found himself waiting to make a left-hand turn at a green light. A semi-truck was blocking his vision. Eventually, the truck driver waved him on, and Aaron turned. Then, BOOM, he was sideswiped, which resulted in a crumpled truck and cracked ribs.

In the weeks that followed, Aaron carried a sadness with him over his totaled truck. About a month after the accident, Aaron opened his mail and found a ticket for the accident. He just looked at me and said, "Wasn't it enough that I lost my truck? This ticket just adds insult to injury."

***

Heavenly Hint

"Let your gentleness be known to everyone. The Lord is near."
Philippians 4:5

***
Reflection

The eighth fruit of the Spirit is gentleness. Gentleness is knowing that we could hurt another person and may even be justified, but we choose to be tender-hearted instead. It is important to be gentle with our children when responding to their mistakes because we love them and do not want to hurt them unnecessarily. We need to remember that we all make mistakes and that we would want people to be gentle with us. One way to do this is by putting ourselves in the other person's shoes. How do we want someone else to respond to our mistakes or the mistakes of our children?

Learning from our mistakes does not always require consequences. There are times when the mistake itself is the lesson, and a gentle response can allow that lesson to sink in. Or a soft response can stop us from hurting our children unnecessarily. In Mary's Memory, Aaron had already learned his lesson when he totaled his truck and cracked his ribs. The ticket mailed to him did only add insult to injury. The same can be true of our children's mistakes. There are times when the mistake in and of itself is the lesson, and gentleness is the better response rather than giving a consequence. Intentionally deciding to look into our hearts and respond with gentleness provides an example to our children of God's gentleness.

Moreover, when our children make a mistake, we want to be careful not to be unkind or say things that might not be correct. For example, when Mary was in second grade, a blonde-haired friend wanted darker hair. Mary tried to help her and decided that putting suntan oil all over her hair would do the trick. She thought that if it could tan skin, then it could tan hair and make it darker too. Mary also believed it would not be permanent because a suntan is not permanent.

When it did not work, Mary was sad, and she felt so bad that she had disappointed her friend. The next thing Mary knew, her mom and the girl's mom were standing before her, angry and upset. Even after Mary explained what she thought would happen, her mom said, "You know better than that." In truth, Mary did not know and was confused as to why she was in trouble. Once she got punished, she felt wronged. As Aaron had put it, it only added insult to injury. Mary had learned from her mistake and would not try it again.

Moms, we want to be careful how we respond when our children make a mistake. Keep in mind that sometimes the mistake is the lesson, as in Aaron's case. Or saying things such as, "You know better than that." or "Why would you do that?" can be hurtful and unnecessary, as in Mary's case.

Saint Paul of the Cross says, "Be gentle in your actions; speak with a peaceful mind and in a calm tone, and you will succeed better." A gentle response is a holy response, for God is gentle when dealing with our mistakes. So, moms, let us use gentleness in our daily encounters with others, especially with our children. When our children make a mistake, take a moment to discern before responding, and then respond in such a way that "your gentleness will be known to everyone.

***

Homework from Heaven

"Teachable Moment"

Consider...

1. Carefully listening to your children when they make a mistake. They might not have known it was wrong, as with Mary when she put sunscreen in her friend's hair. In this case, talk to your children through why what they did was wrong. Use it as a teachable moment.
2. Being gentle regardless of whether a consequence is warranted or not. Shaming children can only make things worse by tearing down both their spirit and your relationship with them.

***
Prayerful Pause

*Dear Holy Spirit,
Help us to be gentle with our children
when they make mistakes. Remind us that
they are still learning.
Amen.*

***
Memos to Me

_____

_____

_____

_____

_____

_____

***
Pondering through Pictures

Keeping Routines

***
Mary's Memory
"Freedom"

When I was a teacher, I established routines in my classroom. It ran like clockwork. At the start of the year, I was staunch about not allowing students to deviate from the routine. This bothered my students and some of my parents. The parents were concerned because their children were frustrated. Not everyone liked me. That was okay with me because I knew that eventually, my students would see that they have more freedom of movement if they just followed the routine.

I did not believe in having students sit at their desks all day. They need the opportunity to move. So, one of my routines had freedom of movement built into it. I had fun learning stations around the room that once students finished their class work and there was still time, my students could participate in those stations either alone or together quietly. At first, the students wanted access anytime, nope, work first was my rule. That frustrated my students. I understood that some students were quicker than others, so I was careful to make time for all students to participate as often as I could.

Between Thanksgiving and Christmas, my classroom became a happy one. The students did come to understand their freedom and that my routine was advantageous. They enjoyed the structured routine because they figured out that it gave them freedom of movement and freedom of choice. The parents also came to appreciate it because their children were happy. The classroom routine produced an atmosphere of peace and calm as everyone was in sync with the flow of each day.

***
Heavenly Hint

*"Instead, I tell you,
be guided by the Spirit, and you will no
longer yield to self-indulgence."
Galatians 5:16*

***
Reflection

The ninth fruit of the Spirit is self-control. Self-control is imperative in a mother's life because the world is filled with chaos. Just watch the news. But families need to maintain a sense of calm in order to thrive. Self-control can do just that because self-control develops and keeps routines. Routines can be difficult, especially when our children want to do something else, but we are strong and can maintain them. In 2 Timothy 1:7 it says, "God did not give us a spirit of timidity, but the Spirit of power and love and self-control." It is indeed important to maintain routines and keep calmness and order so children can thrive. In the memory above, Mary did this in her classroom. Her students knew exactly what to expect each day, which gave them a sense of security. They did not need to experience chaos because routine counters chaos. Routines bring order. What a beautiful thing. God models this for us in many ways in His seasons, the tides, sunrises, and sunsets. God is a God of order because He loves us and wants us to feel the calm that order brings.

When a family, especially the children, knows what to expect, they feel that sense of calm. Routines allow children to thrive because their minds are not anxious about what is coming next. If they know and can count on the routine, it will enable their imaginations to do what they are supposed to do; grow in curiosity, play, and learn. Their bodies rest consistently and eat regularly, while their minds have time for learning, engaging, playing, and praying. It is all a balance for a family, and that balance takes self-control. Saint Anthony of Egypt told us that, "The fruits of the earth are not brought to perfection immediately, but by time, rain and care; similarly, the fruits of men ripen through ascetic practice, study, time, perseverance, self-control and patience." Our children need consistent routines to thrive, much like the fruits of the earth need consistent sunshine and rain to ripen. So, moms, let us create calm and balance in our homes as we stick to our daily routines using the Holy Spirit's fruit of self-control.

***

Homework from Heaven

"The Beauty of Order"

What to Do:
1. Have a discussion with your children about how life would be different if we didn't know when spring, summer, fall, or winter would start or how long they would last.
2. Ask your children how life would be different if we couldn't count on the sun to rise and set every day.
3. Have your children share with you what routines they think could help them.
4. Brainstorm routines that keep a calm home.
5. Mary's mom kept a house routine. Here are some ideas to get the conversation started with your family:

    a. We cleaned the kitchen immediately after supper every night. That way, the next morning it was good to go for school or work with no mess to deal with.
    b. We were expected to put our belongings away so that the house stayed tidy in the common areas, including any bathrooms. This way no one was embarrassed when their friends came over.
    c. Saturday morning was clean-up day. Everyone had

their chores. Some of us worked inside to clean the house while others mowed, weeded, or whatever was needed outside. This way, weekend plans could be made knowing what was expected to be done first.

***

Prayerful Pause

Dear Spirit,
Help us to use Your gift
of self-control by setting and keeping
routines in our households of faith. May
this consistent effort bring balance and
calm to our homes.
Amen.

***
Memos to Me

_____
_____
_____
_____
_____
_____
_____

***
Pondering through Pictures

Holy Fruits

***

Mary's Memory

"Sixteen Years Later"

I was taking my hour break from work and decided to go to reconciliation. I knew time was short but decided to go for it anyway. As I walked into the church's vestibule, I noticed a woman sitting in a wheelchair, looking out the window as if waiting for somebody. I didn't give it much thought.

I entered the church and took the time to pray and prepare my heart for the sacrament. By the time I got in and out, I figured about half an hour had gone by. As I was leaving, I noticed the woman was still sitting there. I looked at her and smiled, momentarily hesitating because I thought it odd that she was still there. I asked if she needed help. She explained that she had been sitting for an hour and needed someone to help her. Her ride was late, and she was concerned that her family would worry. I immediately reached into my purse, pulled out my cell phone, and began making calls for her. I knew I could not just leave her stranded.

No one answered the calls at any of the phone numbers she had given me. I didn't know what to do. I was not wearing a watch, so I didn't know how much of my break remained, but I did know I was running out of time. Something inside said, "Just stay with her." As we sat there, we decided to try calling people again. We began talking, and before we knew it, her ride showed up, apologizing for being so late. I left, and as I walked in through the doors at work, the digital clock turned to the next minute - the very same minute that marked the end of my break.

***

Heavenly Hint

"This is My commandment, that you love one another as I have loved you."
John 15:12

***

Reflection

These twelve Fruits of the Spirit show us how to mirror God's love and in turn, by our example, teach our children how to mirror His love as well. As moms, they also show us how to reflect what we want to see in our children. Remember when Mary and her mom were at the hospital and her mom buttoned the woman's shirt? Mary's mom took courage from the Holy Spirit and used her holy boldness in that situation. Sixteen years later, the actions of Mary's mom influenced Mary enough to embolden her to mirror her mom's love for the woman in the wheelchair, who sat waiting for her ride home from church. Mary's mom mirrored the Holy Spirit's love, and because of her mom's example, Mary had, in turn, learned to mirror God's love.

Let us reflect God's love by bringing the Fruits of the Holy Spirit to our households of faith and to the people around us. Saint Thérèse of Lisieux says, "Let us love, since that is what our hearts were made for." So, moms, let us with intention, live the Holy Spirit's fruits of love, and then along with God, we will smile when we see our children doing the same.

***
Homework from Heaven
"An Apple a Day"/ "Fruit Cards"

Materials: "An Apple a Day"
- Large poster board
- Markers
- Scissors
- Glue
- Multi-colored construction paper or cardstock

What to Do: For Younger Children

The Spirit fills us with His life and love through the Fruits. When we take advantage of the Fruits, we are able to share that love with the world around us. The tree we will be assembling represents the life of the Spirit. The roots bring the life and the nutrients to the fruit it bears. As you assemble the tree, explain this analogy to your children to help them better understand the importance of the Fruits of the Spirit. We are providing a simple way to do this project but be creative. You can use sticks or actual apples cut in half and dipped in paint. God's world is at your disposal on this one. Have fun!

1. At the top of the poster board write the Title: Fruits of the Spirit.
2. Below the title draw a large tree with empty branches.
3. Draw twelve roots coming out from the bottom of the Tree.
4. Write one Fruit of the Spirit on each root. Label each root starting with the words "Rooted in" For example, if you are working on Peace your root would say, "Rooted in Peace."
5. Next, cut out twelve apple shapes from the construction paper - a size that would allow you to put all twelve apples on the tree. At the top of the apple write the name of the fruit, for example, "Peace." Depending on the maturity of

your children, for little ones six years and younger write a list of things your children can do to bring peace to your home. For example, sharing toys, forgiving each other, and praying together. For children ages seven to tenish, have them look up a scripture quote about each fruit. Do this with each fruit as you go. So, as not to overwhelm your child, we recommend doing either one fruit per day or one fruit per week.

6. Glue the apples to the tree.
7. Once done, cut out a few leaves to glue around the apples, or get leaves from outside.
8. Consider putting this poster up in the kitchen or dining room and refer to it whenever you wish. Remind your children that the Fruits of the Spirit are ways to give the Holy Spirit's love to the people around them.

***

Materials: "Fruit Cards"
- Index cards
- Sharpies™

What to Do: For Older Children
1. Give twelve index cards to each of your children.
2. Have them write a Fruit of the Spirit on each card.
3. Laminate the cards for lasting power.
4. Each day, fan out your children's cards and have them draw one.
5. The fruit they select is the Fruit of the Spirit that they will concentrate on for that day. (If they need the help of another gift, make sure they know that it's available.)
6. Repeat until all the cards have been used or continue it as long as you wish.
7. At supper, have each person share which fruit they drew and if they have an example of how that fruit of the Spirit helped them that day.

***
Prayerful Pause

*Dear Holy Spirit,
Thank You for Your Fruits.
May we live by each one carefully and,
therefore, develop a closer relationship
with You and all of those around us.
Amen.*

***
Memos to Me

_____
_____
_____
_____
_____
_____
_____
_____

***
Pondering through Pictures

Women of the Beatitudes

***

*During his Beatification Mass,
Saint Pope Saint John Paul II said of Saint Pier Giorgio:*

*"By his example he proclaims
that a life lived in Christ's Spirit, the Spirit of the Beatitudes, is 'blessed,' and that only the person who becomes a 'man or woman of the Beatitudes' can succeed in communicating love
and peace to others."*

Living with Intention

***

If our aim is to become "Women of the Beatitudes" and "succeed in communicating love and peace to others," then we need to listen to the Spirit's call to know the Beatitudes and to live them with intention. To live them intentionally, we will first have to acknowledge our need for the Spirit. When we couple the Holy Spirit's gifts with the Beatitudes, we fully embrace the "Spirit of the Beatitudes" and are blessed. Here we go!

The Beatitudes

***

"Blessed are the poor in spirit,
for theirs is the Kingdom of Heaven.

Blessed are those who mourn,
for they will be comforted.

Blessed are the meek (gentle), for they will inherit the earth.

Blessed are those who hunger and thirst for righteousness, for they will be filled (satisfied).

Blessed are the merciful, for they will receive mercy.

Blessed are the pure in heart, for they will see God.

Blessed are the peacemakers,
for they will be called children of God.

Blessed are those who are persecuted for righteousness' sake,
for theirs is the Kingdom of Heaven."

Matthew 5:1-12

Be Comforted

***
Mary's Memory
"That Precious Newborn"

When Laurie had her daughter, Rebekah, I couldn't wait to meet the newest Robbins. So, I went down to spend the day helping Laurie. It had only been eight months since I had lost my baby, John Kirby, and when Laurie put that precious newborn in my arms, it all came rushing back. I dropped my head on Rebekah's and started sobbing. How I didn't expect that to happen, I will never know.

Laurie was incredible. Here, I was there to help her, and she was comforting me. By evening, Rebekah began to fuss, and none of my newborn tricks worked. Laurie came over to me and gently said, "Maybe she wants her Mama." It hit me right then that Laurie had not held Rebekah all day. By putting baby Rebekah in my arms and allowing me to love on her, Laurie eased my mourning over losing my baby and gave me solace that day.

***
Heavenly Hint
"Blessed are they who mourn, for they will be comforted." Matthew 5:4

***
Reflection

"Blessed are those who mourn, for they will be comforted" is the second beatitude, and our discussion of it will be quite literal. To understand this beatitude, we need to understand what it means to mourn. One principal reason people mourn is heartache as Mary experienced in her story above. Mourning has no timeline. We grieve in our own way over the losses we go through in our lives. People mourn over different things. What makes one person's heart ache may not affect someone else. What matters is that someone is heartbroken and needs comfort.

This beatitude calls us to empathize with each other, by tuning into another person's emotions, feeling a person's emptiness in life, and sharing in his or her grief. Loving someone enough to be willing to share in their suffering is the inherent blessing of the beatitude and what Laurie and Mary shared in the memory above. Mary still ached for her baby and was therefore blindsided in her enthusiasm to meet Laurie's newborn. Her grief suddenly overwhelmed her because of it but as it says in Psalm 34:18, "Yahweh is near to the broken-hearted, He helps those whose spirit is crushed." The Spirit used Laurie to help Mary. She knew Mary was still mourning the loss of John Kirby, and that day Laurie not only saw but felt Mary's pain and placed Rebekah in Mary's arms in the hope of decreasing the ache in her heart. Jesus blessed Mary as Laurie comforted her that day. Laurie did not stop Mary's mourning forever. No one will ever be able to do that, although that day, Laurie eased it.

At any given time of our lives, we may be the mourner, or we may be the comforter because life happens. There could be a loss as significant as losing a parent or a job or as small as losing a special necklace. What is important is that if we are the mourner, we need to stay open to the blessing that God wants to give us from a comforter and accept it. In the above story, when all the emotions of losing John Kirby came flooding back, Mary could have decided to get up, hand the baby back to Laurie, and leave, but she would have missed out on this beatitude's blessing of a friend's love. On the flip side, the comforter needs to be open to helping the mourner. Laurie could have taken care of Rebekah, but instead, she saw Mary's anguish and chose to comfort her; therefore, she too received a blessing, for she felt joy in being able to lighten Mary's heavy heart.

The Holy Spirit's gift of wisdom enables us to bring God's love into our daily lives and our relationships with others. Pope Francis says, "They (We) discover the meaning of life by coming to the aid of those who suffer, understanding their anguish and bringing relief." Let us turn to the Holy Spirit's gift of wisdom and be unafraid to comfort those who mourn, as well as accept the comfort of others when we are grieving ourselves.

***

Homework from Heaven

"Grieving Again"

What to Do:

1. Stay open to times when your children re-grieve over a loss they've had earlier in life.
2. For example, Mary lost her grandpa in second grade. She didn't know her grandpa, so she didn't feel sad for herself but remembered feeling sad because her mom was sad. When she was around twelve, her older brother told her a story about her grandpa. Afterward, Mary went to her room and cried. It dawned on her that she never got the opportunity to know her grandpa because they lived in different states, and now she never would. Mary was re-grieving.
3. There are numerous things children can re-grieve over. It can be as small as a teddy bear or as big as losing someone they love. It all depends on the age and developmental maturity of the child. In second grade, Mary did not understand her loss, but by seventh grade she did.

4. Stay aware and remain empathetic, even if it doesn't make sense to you, because your child is still hurting.

***

Prayerful Pause

Dear Holy Spirit,
Please give us Your wisdom to have an empathetic heart, prepared to help those who mourn, and an open heart to accept those who want to comfort us.
Amen.

***
Memos to Me

_____
_____
_____
_____
_____
_____
_____

***
Pondering through Pictures

Inherit the Earth

***

Laurie's Story

"Why?"

We had just moved into our new house when our next-door neighbor immediately tested us with "love thy neighbor" by familiarizing us with the following:

When the neighbor's old fence breaks, the Robbins must fix it.
Why? I don't know, but we acquiesced.

If a Robbins' ball goes over the fixed fence, it goes into the trash!
Why? I don't know, but balls can be replaced.

If a Robbins' ball hits the fence, the Sheriff "Might just get a call!"
Why? I don't know, but balls can be kicked in the other direction.

If the Robbins go out to play, the neighbor's music is up all day.
Why? I can guess, but we enjoy listening to music.

If the Robbins give the neighbor flowers, they land in the trash.
Why? I don't know; perhaps the balls were getting lonely.

When Jesus said, "Love thy neighbor,"
the Robbins didn't ask ~ Why?

***
Heavenly Hint

*"Blessed are the meek (gentle),
for they will inherit the earth."*
Matthew 5:5

***
Reflection

The next beatitude is, "Blessed are the meek (gentle), for they will inherit the earth." The gentle bear no grudges and are not provoked to anger. They do not have to "win" because the gentle are inwardly strong. In the story above, Steve and Laurie were gentle with a neighbor who regularly provoked them. In their frustration, it would have been easy for Steve and Laurie to hold a grudge or try to get back at their neighbor; but they did not. Instead, they chose gentleness. They lived what scripture tells us in Leviticus 19:18, "You shall not take vengeance or bear a grudge against any of your people, but you shall love your neighbor as yourself…"

When frustrated, choosing gentleness demonstrates God's love because gentleness refrains from hurting the other person. As Saint John Bosco says, "Gentleness… is the favorite virtue of Jesus Christ." That is because Jesus does not want us to hurt one another. When we get frustrated, it is easy to become momentarily self-centered. We want our way; we want to "win," but if we win, someone else loses. We cannot risk teaching our children that it is okay to force a win regardless of the other person's feelings, to alleviate our own feelings of frustration.

Choosing to be gentle will take the Holy Spirit's gift of piety. Piety is devotion to God. Devotion means being in a loyal, loving relationship with someone and doing what it takes to stay connected to them. Piety will help us not bear grudges and be gentle in times of frustration, especially when dealing with our children, who are at our mercy. When we are devoted to God, we do not want to separate ourselves from Him by hurting others. When frustrated, we can become self-centered, thus disconnecting us from God and from those we love. So, mothers, let us turn to the Holy Spirit's gift of piety to help us choose gentleness in our vocation of motherhood.

***

Homework from Heaven

"Neighborly Love"

What to Do:
Take the time to build a friendship with your neighbors. Goodwill can go a long way to bring joy to our lives. It's nice to know that there are people around you that you can rely on or be that person that your neighbors can count on. If there's an elderly neighbor, check on them and help them when needed. If there is a mother with young children, look for ways to encourage her or give her a break by having her kids come over to your house to play. You can bring a meal or dessert for either one. Encourage barbeques in the summer and Christmas parties or caroling in the winter. The point is to make time for your neighbors.

***

Prayerful Pause

Dear Holy Spirit,
Please give us Your gift of piety to help
keep our nature gentle and our
devotion to You strong.
Amen.

*** Memos to Me

_____
_____
_____
_____
_____
_____
_____

*** Pondering through Pictures

Be Satisfied

***

Laurie's Story

"Carrying Your Cross"

Throughout our journey as friends and prayer partners, Mary and I have discovered that both prayer and action are necessary in life. We provide balance for each other. I frequently call Mary to prayer and she, in turn, calls me to action. We will demonstrate this balance with a very familiar symbol. This symbol has two beams, one is vertical, and the other is horizontal. The vertical beam represents our prayer life. The horizontal beam represents our service to others and God. When balanced correctly, these two beams make a perfect cross. Alone, Mary and I were off balance. To borrow from The Beatitudes, Mary and I both hungered and thirsted for righteousness, but neither one of us was satisfied because I prayed but sometimes failed to take action and Mary took action but sometimes failed to first pray.

I had firmly planted my vertical beam by reaching up to God in prayer for others. That was my first response. Sometimes, I would forget the importance of connecting to God in heaven by serving others. On the other hand, Mary had held her horizontal beam by reaching out in service to others. That was her first response. Sometimes, she would forget the importance of connecting to God in heaven by clasping her hands in prayer. Over the years, I have reminded Mary to adjust her first response by planting her vertical beam firmly in prayer, thus connecting to God differently. Now when she serves, she believes she is following God's will. Mary has encouraged me to adjust my first response by carrying my horizontal beam firmly in service, thus connecting to God differently. Now when I pray, my prayer leads me to take action in the service of God. God took a wonderful friendship and prayer partnership and created two moms who no longer rely on half a cross, they each now carry a complete cross. The combination of prayer and action is crucial because it will take both prayer and action to bring about the Kingdom of God right here on earth.

***

Heavenly Hint

"Blessed are they who hunger and thirst for righteousness, for they will be filled (satisfied)."
Matthew 5:6

***

Reflection

The next beatitude is "Blessed are they who hunger and thirst for righteousness, for they will be filled (satisfied)." Those who hunger and thirst for righteousness want the Kingdom of God in their lives and the lives of others. They seek justice in our world. They want wrongs righted and to help those who cannot help themselves. This desire to help is a call to love, which is a verb. Love is a call to action.

Once we understand our call, we use our understanding of righteousness to guide our actions. Our actions will need to be twofold: one to pray and two to act. Injustice and sin fill the world. It will require us to pray and act to change this so that the Kingdom of God will be right here on earth. While we cannot fix everything, we can surely do our part by acting on what we are passionate about. There could be a time when God will say to us, as He did to Moses in Exodus 14:15, "Why do you cry out to me? Tell the Israelites to go forward." For some going forward, that could be helping in a soup kitchen; for others, it could be providing a safe place for children when their parents are at work. Achieving God's will necessitates both prayer and action.

As moms, it is necessary to teach our children to both pray and act. We cannot risk allowing them to think it is alright to stand by quietly when they see an injustice. When they see an injustice, we should lead them to pray about it and then guide them in action to address it. As Saint Augustine once said, "Pray as if everything depended on God. Work as if everything depended on you." Saint Augustine is sharing some serious wisdom here, and the Holy Spirit's gift of fortitude will help us along the way.

Our world is far from perfect, and many injustices could take years to address. We will need the Holy Spirit's help to persevere. His gift of fortitude will do just that because the Holy Spirit's gift of fortitude enables our children and us to be steadfast in our pursuit of the Kingdom of God right here on earth.

***

Homework from Heaven

"Is This Just?"

Materials:
- Candy that your family enjoys
- A medium-sized bowl
- One small-sized bowl for each family member

What to Do:
1. Gather your family.
2. Give each person their bowl.
3. In front of everyone, pour all the candy into the medium bowl.
4. Begin distributing the candy into the smaller individual bowls. As you hand out the candy, exaggerate an unjust distribution.
5. Give one person one piece of candy, another three, and still

another a cupful. Make sure someone gets so much, that their bowl is overflowing.
6. It won't be necessary to ask, is this just? We are confident that you'll hear, "That's not fair. They have more than me."
7. Explain that each person is a country in the world. Some countries have lots of food, like the United States; others have very little, like Africa. This activity will demonstrate the injustice that some have food, and some do not in a world with enough food for everyone. Teach your children that when we see injustice, or something happening that is wrong in the world, God calls us to do what we can to stop it. That does not mean acting impulsively. It takes prayer and a plan.
8. Pray in thanksgiving for the candy and distribute it equally.
9. Discuss some of the injustices your children see or endure in their daily lives or in the world. Choose as a family something you want to work on together. Pray with one another and come up with a plan to right what it is you have chosen to address.

***

Prayerful Pause

Dearest Holy Spirit,
Please give us the fortitude necessary to live a lifetime of prayer and action.
Amen.

***
Memos to Me

―――――――――――――――――――――――――
―――――――――――――――――――――――――
―――――――――――――――――――――――――
―――――――――――――――――――――――――
―――――――――――――――――――――――――
―――――――――――――――――――――――――
―――――――――――――――――――――――――
―――――――――――――――――――――――――

***
Pondering through Pictures

Receive Mercy

***

Laurie's Story

"Thank You"

My daughter, Sarah, had planned to go to a friend's house and make brownies. Her friend did not have the fixings, so Sarah asked me if we could stop at the store on the way to her house. I agreed, and we were off. Once in the store, we picked up a brownie mix and a few other groceries that I needed. Since we only had a few items, Sarah and I decided to go through the self-checkout to make it quicker.

Once we finished putting the groceries through the scanners, I pulled out what I thought was my debit card and tried to pay several times, but the machine did not authorize my card. The checkout person helping in the area saw me having difficulty and told me to come down to his machine and that he would help me. We tried the card again with the same result. Without hesitation, he pulled his wallet out, took out his card, and paid for my groceries. I was so surprised. I told him how grateful I was for his generosity. We left, and I dropped Sarah off at her friend's house. I then went back home, got the right card, and returned to the store so that I could repay the gentleman who had helped me.

On my way into the store, I noticed that he was sitting out front. I figured he was on his break and hoped I could catch him before he returned to work. So, I dashed into the store, got the money out of the ATM, and brought it out to him. He did not accept it. He simply said to me, "No, you're good." and smiled. I asked, "Are you sure?" He replied, "Yes." I thanked him and went on my way.

The following day, I picked up my mom so we could run some errands together. While driving, we noticed a young family sitting together on the sidewalk next to the road. They had a sign indicating that they needed help. It was then that it dawned on me that I still had that cash. So, as I pulled over to help, I quickly explained to Mom what had happened the day before.

Once stopped, I took the money out of my purse and gave it to my mom. She rolled the window down to hand it to the father approaching the car. After she gave him the money, the father smiled and said thank you. He continued facing us as he walked back to his family, putting the money to his chest. He had a look of such gratefulness in his eyes, and that touched us. I only hope that the gentleman who had helped me saw that same look in mine.

***

Heavenly Hint

*"Blessed are the merciful,
for they will receive mercy."
Matthew 5:7*

***

Reflection

The next beatitude is "Blessed are the merciful, for they will receive mercy." Mercy is grounded in having compassion for someone who needs help. However, mercy goes a step beyond in that we choose to act upon our feeling of compassion by helping people we see in need. Mercy compels us to help people willingly for mercy unites us with the will of Jesus. Pope Francis explained this when he said, "The fruits of profound union with Jesus are marvelous: our whole being is transformed by the grace of the Holy Spirit, intelligence, will, affections, and even the body, because we are united in body and spirit." When we are united with Jesus our actions are led by His Spirit. Jesus is mercy itself, and His mercy moves through us and thereby blesses us.

The Holy Spirit has a gift to help us be merciful. His gift of counsel will lead us. When we listen to the Holy Spirit He guides our actions. Laurie's story above shows this. The gentleman in the store was merciful by generously paying for her groceries. In turn, Laurie could have kept that cash she had pulled from the ATM. Instead, she listened to the Holy Spirit and was inspired to act mercifully by giving the money to the family sitting on the roadside. One of the lovely things about this story is the acknowledgment that Laurie did not only help someone else, but she also accepted help herself. One of the keys to becoming a merciful person is to accept that everyone, including us, will need help at some point.

Sometimes, it is difficult to accept help from others as well as give it. Our pride can get in the way. However, if we listen to the Holy Spirit's gift of counsel it can help us with our pride because He will guide us to look beyond ourselves and accept help or give help to others. Pope Francis tells us that counsel, "is the gift with which the Holy Spirit helps us to make decisions in our concrete lives, following the logic of Jesus and His gospel... God enlightens our hearts and directs our thoughts, words and actions in accordance with His saving will." Let us remember that Jesus is mercy Himself and reveals this throughout His gospels. Moms, may we be open to both giving and receiving mercy, in so doing, allowing ourselves and others to obtain God's mercy, thus bringing the Kingdom of God right here on earth.

***

Homework from Heaven

"A Neighbor in Need, Calls for Mercy Indeed"

What to Do:

Teach our children to be merciful people by encouraging compassionate behavior. Here is a list of ways of helping our children to go beyond compassion to action by having them:

1. Mow the lawn or water the flowers for someone they know who cannot do it for him/herself.
2. Go grocery shopping with someone who cannot get there alone.
3. Cook a meal for a neighbor/friend who is struggling.
4. Walk the dog for a neighbor/friend who needs help.
5. Visit an elderly person they know who could be lonely.
6. Do the Christmas shopping and/or wrapping for someone who cannot do it for him/herself.
7. Pay attention to their neighbors/friends and help when they hear a need.

The list can go on and on. Trust the Holy Spirit to inspire merciful action where needed.

***

Prayerful Pause

*Dear Holy Spirit,
Remind us to seek Your counsel when we feel compassion toward others in need and compel us to act in a meaningful way to help them.
Amen.*

***
Memos to Me

_____
_____
_____
_____
_____
_____
_____

***
Pondering through Pictures

See God

***

Laurie's Story

"A Smiling Friend"

I had returned home from the hospital after giving birth and was holding my newborn Rebekah Grace. It was a tough transition beginning a new home life, not just because I had five children under the age of nine, but because my little two-year-old, Bethie Boo, begged me to hold her every time she saw me. I was feeling overwhelmed by it all when suddenly there was a knock at my door. "What now?" I thought. As I opened the door, there stood a young man from Steve's youth group. To my surprise, he said, "Steve has done so much for the youth group that I thought I would stop by and see if you needed help with anything." My response was a quick one, "Please come in." - He did, and he continued to for the next seven months. Once or twice a week, I found a smiling friend working around my house. This boy's offer of help moved me. His humility and willingness to serve touched my heart and eased my burden.

***

Heavenly Hint

"Blessed are the pure of heart, for they will see God."
Matthew 5:8

***
Reflection

"Blessed are the pure in heart, for they will see God" is the next beatitude. The pure in heart are those who do not try to serve God and their own self-interests at the same time. The pure in heart know this and are sincere in their actions. They can be themselves without pretense. They know God's goodness and, with their pure heart, listen to the Spirit and intentionally spread His goodness to the world around them. Saint Augustine tells us, "God bestows more consideration on the purity of the intention with which our actions are performed then on the actions themselves."

In Proverbs 20:11 says, "A young man's character appears in what he does, if his behavior is pure and straight." Such a young man appears in Laurie's Story above. God's goodness came through the young man who helped Laurie. He recognized how much Steve had done for both him and the youth group, and in return, wanted to do something for Laurie's family. Knowing that Laurie just had a baby, he came over to help her. The young man was sincere. He had no ulterior motives and simply came to help Laurie. He did not care what he was asked to do. Rather, he just did it with a pure heart filled with love for God. Through his pure heart, Laurie could see God.

The Holy Spirit's gift of wisdom will help us to be pure in heart. For His wisdom keeps our hearts and minds focused on Him. With our hearts and minds focused on God, our own self-interests fall away, and we can live our lives with a pure heart prepared to serve Him.

***
Homework from Heaven
"Safeguarding the Innocent"

What to Do:

In today's world, children are growing up fast. We encourage you to protect your children's minds and hearts for as long as possible. Part of maintaining a pure heart is by giving information at the appropriate age. Childhood and its innocence only come along once. Once it is gone, it is gone forever. You can't go back. So, know that it's okay to shield your children. Don't let the world bully you into believing you are overprotective and that it's wrong to safeguard your children's innocence because it's not.

***

Prayerful Pause

*Dear Holy Spirit,
May we seek Your wisdom so that our hearts and motives remain pure in all we do for Your glory.
Amen.*

***
Memos to Me

_____
_____
_____
_____
_____
_____
_____

***
Pondering through Pictures

Be the Children of God

***

Laurie's Story

"Best Car I Ever Had!"

My dad was dropping off my brother James to his basketball practice in our 1972 dark green Plymouth Duster. The boys had nicknamed it "The Dragon" because of its color. It was an old car, but it got everyone where they needed to be. Upon getting out of the car, one of the coaches suddenly approached James and said to him, "I wouldn't be caught dead in a car like that!" No sooner had he said this when another coach walked up who had apparently heard the coach's rude comment because he rebutted, "Is that a Plymouth Duster? I had one of those in college - best car I ever had!"

***

Heavenly Hint

*"Blessed are the peacemakers,
for they will be called children of God."*
Matthew 5:9

***

Reflection

The next beatitude is "Blessed are the peacemakers, for they will be called children of God." Can you imagine what the world would be like if more of us were peacemakers, like the second coach in Laurie's story above? The first coach's comment was uncalled for, but the second coach's comment helped Laurie's brother and hopefully made the first coach think about his actions. Saint Teresa of Calcutta would be proud of this coach because she once said, "Spread love everywhere you go, let no one ever come to you without leaving better and happier." The second coach saw that the first coach had hurt both James and Laurie's dad with his words and brought peace to the situation with a bit of levity. He did as Saint Teresa of Calcutta suggested by allowing both James and Laurie's dad to leave feeling "better and happier."

People are too quick to give their opinion on social media in today's world because they cannot see the other person. When we are two different people, by behaving one way in front of people and another way behind our screen or treating our family kindly when our friends are around and less than kindly when our friends are gone, we certainly have an angel and a devil on our shoulders, don't we? [15]A character in Batman is named Two-Face. When making a decision, he leaves it up to fate. In his mind, there is no right or wrong and the pursuit of peace has nothing to do with it. However, to the rest of us, peace does have something to do with it because our decisions can hurt others. We should teach our children this because Romans 12:18 tells us, "As much as possible, and to the utmost of your ability, be at peace with everyone."

So, moms, let us teach our children to always behave in a right and just manner, for acting like Two-Face makes it easier to legitimize wrong behavior. At least with Two-Face, there is a shot at peace. But when we behave one way in front of people and another behind our screen or treat our family kindly with friends and not so much when friends are gone, we destroy peace.

Peacemakers always behave the same way because they know the importance of people and their dignity at all times. Peacemakers do not injure people. They both model and promote benevolence. They desire the best for others and show it in both word and deed. Saint Teresa of Calcutta reminds us that, "If we have no peace, it is because we have forgotten that we belong to each other." The Holy Spirit's gift of Fear of the Lord will help us with this. Our fear of the Lord comes from knowing God's awesome greatness. Children of God know this and revere God and, therefore, love and respect His people. That is what peacemakers do, spread love and respect throughout the Kingdom of God right here on earth.

***

Homework from Heaven

"Peacemaker or Buttinski?"

What to Do:

Teach your children to be peacemakers. Remember to teach your children that there's a fine line between being a peacemaker and being a buttinski. A peacemaker is looking out for everyone's best interests, while a buttinski is someone who meddles where they do not belong. Here are five steps to help teach your children how to be a peacemaker and not a buttinski. We encourage you to modify them based on the age of your children. Have them ask themselves:

1. "Am I safe to get involved?" If not, leave and get help.
2. "Are others safe?" If not, leave and get help.
3. "Is it any of my business?" In order to determine this, ask yourself these questions:

    a. Does it have anything to do with me?
    b. Will my taking action make it worse?

4. These two questions measure whether or not your child is crossing the line to buttinski rather than being a peacemaker.
5. If your child has determined they can help, then teach them to take a moment to evaluate what is happening. What's causing the conflict?

    a. Decide how to help before intervening.

b. Do you see a compromise you can encourage that will make a difference?
   c. Do you see a potential solution that those in the conflict are missing?

6. Try to be the peacemaker, and if it goes south, either step back or get help if necessary.

***

Prayerful Pause

*Dear Holy Spirit,
Help us hold firm to our
fear of the Lord so that we are the kind of
people who desire the best for others and
seek peace in the process.
Amen.*

***
Memos to Me

_____
_____
_____
_____
_____
_____
_____

***
Pondering through Pictures

Kingdom of Heaven

***

Laurie's Story

"Keeping Our Cool"

When my daughter, Amy was in seventh grade at the local Catholic school, I co-coached the girls' basketball team with another parent. We were at an away game, and our opponent had a reputation for playing dirty. Rumor had it that they didn't think twice about whether or not they hurt someone. This concerned us because the other team's girls were bigger and stronger than our girls.

As the game got started, we quickly discovered that their reputation proved true. Our opponents poked fun at and then laughed at our girls while they blatantly cheated. Shockingly, we found that the refs turned a blind eye to it. It got so bad that we were genuinely concerned that someone would get hurt. A case in point, Amy kept stealing the ball from their biggest player. That player got fed up and when Amy got the ball from her again, she suddenly picked Amy up, shook her, and slammed her back down. My fellow coach and I looked at each other in disbelief. No foul was called. We called for a timeout. Thankfully, Amy was not hurt.

To call my co-coach heated would be an understatement. During the timeout, he suggested that the girls start playing rough back. I reminded him that we represent a Catholic school and that we need to keep our cool and continue to play fairly. As soon as he heard what I said, he immediately agreed, and so did the girls. Amy's team lost that game badly, but we all walked out with our heads held high because we knew we had represented our school, ourselves, and our God well.

***

Heavenly Hint

"Blessed are those who are persecuted for righteousness' sake, for theirs is the Kingdom of Heaven."
Matthew 5:10

***

Reflection

The final beatitude is "Blessed are those who are persecuted for the righteousness' sake, for theirs is the Kingdom of Heaven." To put it simply, being persecuted for the sake of righteousness means when times are tough, we stay true to God's Spirit and stand up for what we know is right. The Holy Spirit's gift of knowledge will help us know what is right from what is wrong. With His help, we are better able to make sound judgments.

In Laurie's story, the other team was cheating, and it would have been easy to cheat back, but cheating is wrong, regardless of the circumstances. Our relationship with God always comes first. When we do what is right, we live for God. It does not matter what the people around us are saying or doing.

How do we behave righteously? We strive to act justly in all situations. That means fighting the desire to conform when we know something wrong is happening, especially when it would be easier or make us happier to comply. Let us look at what Saint Augustine said, [16]"Conformity is doing what everyone else is doing, regardless of what is right. Morality is doing what is right, regardless of what everyone else is doing." This concept can be difficult for children from ages three to ninety-three. We are all God's children, and we all fight peer pressure despite our age.

As we raise our children, it is necessary that we live out our faith because, as Saint Toribio reminds us, "Christ said, 'I am the

Truth;' He did not say, 'I am the custom.'" Times change, as today's youth like to tell us, but truth and righteousness do not, as they come from the Holy Spirit. The Spirit will keep reminding us of this with His gift of knowledge through prayer and scripture. For example, in Romans 12:2, He reminds us, "Do not be conformed to this world, but be transformed by the renewing of your minds, so that you may discern what is the will of God - what is good and acceptable and perfect." When we teach our children that it is good to suffer persecution for the sake of righteousness, we will be leading them toward the Kingdom of Heaven.

What do we mean by asking our children to suffer persecution? We ask them to, in all situations, ask themselves if what is happening around them is right and good. If not, they should not participate in it, even if their peers want them to. That is difficult. It means they will have to be careful about the friends they keep. Our children's friends will strongly influence them. If they have friends who share their values, it will be much easier to live by God's truth and not the world's customs.

The friends that we keep help us to live righteous lives because when times get rough or in difficult situations, they share our values and will help us to stay true to God's Spirit and stand up for what we know is right. The Holy Spirit's gift of knowledge will help us, for He will guide us to God's truth at all times.

***

Homework from Heaven

"Stories of the Saints"

What to Do:

Stories of the saints provide us with many beautiful examples of standing up for what is right in the face of persecution. The saints are people who put God first in their lives and do what is right no matter what. Their stories can help us and our children gain confidence in living out our faith by using the talents and gifts God gave us to draw others closer to Him. Saint

Catherine of Sienna tells us, "Be who God meant you to be, and you will set the world on fire." Consider finding stories that you think will especially resonate with your children.

***

Prayerful Pause

*Dear Holy Spirit,
Please give us the knowledge to know what is right and the strength to stand up for it, despite the repercussions.
Amen.*

***
Memos to Me

***
Pondering through Pictures

Final Thoughts

***

*"Have I (God) not told you:
Be strong and stand firm? Be fearless and
undaunted, for go where you may,
Yahweh your God is with you."
Joshua 1:9*

Trust in Me

***

Mary's Memory

"New Year's Bike Ride"

It was New Year's Day. The sun was shining, and my son, Patrick and I decided to go for a bike ride. Patrick had set a goal the previous autumn to take the training wheels off his bike. He remembered this goal and asked, "Can I ride without my training wheels?" I said, "Sure." During the bike ride, Patrick discovered that going down hills was a little scarier than he thought. You see, as we rode back towards home, there was a slight hill of maybe twelve feet leading directly to a pretty well-traveled street. Patrick stopped in fear. I rode down the hill and stopped at the crosswalk, waiting for Patrick to ride down and reassured him, saying, "Trust me, just use your brakes, and if you get going too fast, I will stop you. See, my bike is blocking the street." Patrick paused and looked at me trepidatiously, then started down. My heart was full as Patrick came to a controlled stop right beside me. As we continued our ride home, Patrick exuded joy.

***

Heavenly Hint

*"When I am afraid,
I put my trust in You..."*
Psalm 56:3

***

Reflection

Trusting God is not always easy, especially when we are afraid of what He is asking us to do and we feel vulnerable, just as Patrick did at the top of the hill that New Year's Day. Patrick could trust Mary because her love for him had proven herself worthy of his trust. We can trust God even more than Patrick trusted Mary. God makes no mistakes. Therefore, He will always be trustworthy and love us beyond measure. As Saint Edith Stein tells us, "Lay all your cares about the future trustingly in God's hands and let yourself be guided by the Lord just like a little child." So, Moms, make the time to build a solid friendship with the Blessed Trinity and, with fresh eyes, begin a new journey with the One True God. You will never regret it.

Start by reintroducing yourself to the Father, our Creator. Thank Him for creating you in His image. Adore Him and worship Him. Allow Him to create new tomorrows filled with love and life in abundance, starting with your household of faith.

Next, reintroduce yourself to Jesus, our Savior. Thank Him for opening the gates of heaven. Adore Him and worship Him. Allow Him to love and serve others through you and forgive as readily as He does, starting with your household of faith.

Finally, reintroduce yourself to the Holy Spirit, our Counselor. Thank Him for His remarkable gifts that guide us along our faith journey. Adore Him and worship Him. Let Him empower you in His call to action, starting with your household of faith.

***

Homework from Heaven

"Trust Enough to Try"

What to Do:

Pursue something you know your child is interested in but is fearful of trying. Take the time to invite your child to participate in this activity with you. For example, you could ride bikes together, rollerblade, practice jumping off the diving board together, etc. The world's an open door; just walk through it with your child.

***

Prayerful Pause

Dear God,
I will always trust in You.
Amen.

***
Memos to Me

_____
_____
_____
_____
_____
_____
_____

***
Pondering through Pictures

This is the Day

***

Mary's Memory

"Melancholy Moment"

I recently found myself reflecting on the seasons of my life, thinking back to when my son, Patrick turned thirteen, a teenager. My daughter, Kathleen turned ten, double digits, and Maggie, my youngest daughter, entered kindergarten. These were milestone years for each one of my children.

My children's milestones were such a big deal to me back then and always made me feel a little sad and hungry for each season to stick around a little longer. However, those feelings never last for long. They give way to the joy of discovering the new person emerging before me as they get a little older and change. While I miss who they were and some of the things we used to do together, my children's new interests and curiosities are so wonderful to be a part of. I continue to cherish each stage of my children's lives.

The seasons of my life keep changing, as they are supposed to. I like to remind myself to revel in each one because they are fleeting. I also need to be grateful for each one and love like there is no tomorrow.

***

Heavenly Hint

"For everything there is a season, and a time for every matter under heaven..."
Ecclesiastes 3:1

***

Reflection

Just before dawn, it is dark, quiet, and full of mystery. What lies in front of you? What sits beside you? What stands behind you? Without light, you do not know. Gently a spark appears, slowly, peacefully. God bestows His light with the rising sun. What loveliness has happened here? What possibilities shine with the break of dawn?

"This is the day that the Lord has made; let us rejoice and be glad in it."
Psalm 118:24

Moms, too often we cannot see past the next dirty diaper, or how much time we have before the next nap, or if we can get to the grocery store after work and still get supper made before our child's soccer game. We are so caught up in the moments of living that we forget to look at our life. We can be so wrapped up in taking care of the next task on our to-do list that we do not take the time to look at the opportunities the Lord places before us. Do we seek God? When the answer is no, then we are in darkness without God's light. He shows us with every sunrise that His glorious light shines every day. God sees endless possibilities for each of us. When we can see only an inch past our own life, God sees an eternity. He knows what is lying in front of us and hopes for us to take advantage of it. With each rising sun, God gives us the gift of today. It teems with possibilities. What will you do with it?

> *"This is the day that the Lord has made;*
> *let us rejoice and be glad in it."*
> *Psalm 118:24*

***

Homework from Heaven

"The Rising Sun"

What to Do:
1. Take your household of faith to watch the sunrise.
2. Praise God and thank Him for the day.
3. Simply spend time together in quiet as you watch God's magnificent glory unfold before you.
4. Once the sun has risen, have your family talk about the possibilities they see for your family's future. Ask each other, "What hopes and dreams do you hold in your heart?"
5. When finished, have a scrumptious breakfast, and rejoice together in the day the Lord has made.

***

Prayerful Pause

Dear Father, Son, and Spirit,
Thank You for the gift of today. May we
live it to the fullest, appreciating every
new opportunity You place before us.
Amen.

***
Memos to Me

_____
_____
_____
_____
_____
_____
_____

***
Pondering through Pictures

Closing

Moms, we would like to remind you of Saint Robert Bellarmine's words in the Opening, "The school of Christ is the school of love. On the last day, when the general examination takes place... love will be the whole syllabus." If the whole syllabus is love, then our vocation is to go forth and do our homework well, by freely sharing God's love in our households of faith.

We invite you to fold your hands and bow your head. Pray in thanksgiving for the children the Blessed Trinity has given you to love, now and for all eternity.

***

"To end then...
we wish you joy; try to grow perfect;
encourage one another; have a common
mind and live in peace, and the God of love
and peace will be with you.
The grace of the Lord Jesus Christ,
the love of God and the fellowship of the
Holy Spirit be with you all."
2 Corinthians 13:11,13

May God bless you today,
tomorrow, and always.

Laurie & Mary

***
Memos to Me

***
Pondering through Pictures

Epilogue

***

*"Honor your father and mother;
also, you shall love your
neighbor as yourself."
Matthew 19:19*

Learning to Love

***

We want to honor our moms and dads by sharing a little bit of their life experiences. We will share how they met each other, started their families, and raised us. We both have parents who taught us how to love our God, our family, and our neighbors. The memoirs you are about to read share how our histories have helped mold us into the people we are today and how they prepared us for becoming moms.

Raised to Praise

***

Laurie's Story

"Growing with Grace"

I was born on May 14, 1965, in Omaha, Nebraska, which is where my dad grew up. Dad was a gentle soul who loved to laugh but knew how to get things done. He was raised in the Catholic faith, and he held it dear. It meant so much to him that he decided to enter the seminary after high school. Dad spent his first two years in the seminary, and while there, he discerned that God was calling him to a different vocation. At that point in time, my dad knew he would be drafted, so he voluntarily joined the army and was stationed at Fort Lewis in Washington State, where he spent the next three years. Dad settled into the church on Post and joined a Catholic Young Adult Group off Post. My mom happened to belong to that very same group.

Mom was born in Minnesota, but her family moved to Washington State when she was young. Mom was raised in a large Catholic family with an older sister and four younger brothers. She grew up on a small farm in Olympia. Mom had farm chores, house chores, and school, so she learned how to manage her time well. Mom has always had a great sense of humor. She has told me many times, "Thank goodness God gave me a sense of humor. Otherwise, I'd be dead in a corner somewhere." She was a daddy's girl and always looked forward to her dad coming home from work. Mom's parents were both raised Catholic. Three of my mom's aunts and uncles went into religious life - two became nuns, and one became a priest. Mom remembers her aunts letting her try on their habits and always encouraging mom toward religious life. While Mom did love her faith, she knew she wasn't called to that life. Sure enough, she was right, for she would soon meet a man who would change her life forever.

The day my mom and dad met, the young adult group was having a picnic, and a gentleman from the group had asked Mom to go with him. She wasn't interested - but as parents sometimes do, they encouraged Mom to go, and she acquiesced. Once there, while sitting at a picnic table, Mom saw a new guy coming up over the hill, whose good looks caught her eye. Before Dad and the gal who had brought him had a chance to sit down, Mom approached Dad and asked if that was his girlfriend. When he shook his head no, Mom was undeniably smitten and offered Dad a potato chip. My dad accepted not only the chip but, over time, her heart. And seven months later, he asked for her hand in marriage.

Dad finished his commitment to the army and married my mom in Washington State. After the wedding, they boarded the train headed for Omaha. As they had no place to live, they moved in with my dad's mom. After just two days, Dad declared to my mom, "We need to get jobs." So, my dad got a job with the Omaha Public Power District, and my mom landed a job at the University of Nebraska doing secretarial work. It wasn't long before they learned they were expecting my oldest brother, Bob. Mom left the university and after giving birth to Bob, welcomed Larry, Me, James, Jennifer, and Stephanie over the course of the next ten years.

After fifteen years of being away from her family, Mom was longing for home. In the last of those fifteen years, Dad had lost his childhood friend to brain cancer and struggled to live in the city that held so many memories. Dad announced one day out of the blue, "We're moving to Washington State." So, they put their house up for sale and sold it in one day. Then, my mom found out that she was pregnant. They had to be out of the house in two weeks, so they rented a place close by so that we kids could finish out the school year. Mom and Dad had to make their move quickly in order to get settled before Matt came along. It was not an easy transition, but Mom and Dad welcomed their seventh child with open arms. Mom always said, "Together, all nine of us make an entire baseball team all by ourselves!"

By moving from Nebraska to Washington, Dad had

sacrificed his seniority in the power company and was hired as a meter reader, thus, having to start his fifteen-year career over. On the salary of a meter reader, Dad could not sustain our family. Dad got a second job during the week and a janitorial position on Saturdays to make ends meet. Getting alone time with Dad was precious among us kids. So, to get mine, I spent some Saturdays being a janitor with him, cleaning the school rooms and staff rooms at Sacred Heart Catholic church. While my siblings and I might have sought out time with Dad, we always knew that he would give us time each evening when he got home from work. We always had a family dinner where my parents took an interest in our day. We would visit as a family and connect with Dad and each other before Dad turned his attention to the ever-present projects on his to-do list.

A huge memory of my dad was how he worked so hard to build our house. Because Dad wasn't able to find a job right away, he couldn't get a loan to buy a home. Mom and Dad could only afford to have the outer frame of our two-story house built, and because of this, Dad would have to finish the rest himself. Given the tight finances, Dad could only buy a few materials at a time, so the process took years.

Once completed and as finances eased, Dad gave our family joy by building three additional buildings on our property. One we named "The Cabin," which was a pioneer playhouse for the grandkids. Then came "The Summer House" for my mom to get away and relax. Dad's final masterpiece, which Mom called "The Barn," was a beautiful place with an old-fashioned porch, which he built as a distraction after losing their oldest son, Bob, at fifty. Dad was the definition of a provider who happily did what was necessary to take care of his family.

When my dad wasn't working on the house, he was usually out working on our old cars, repairing and maintaining them for all of us kids. He made sure we all had transportation to get to school, our sports, and our jobs. Sometimes, if Dad couldn't get a car going for a few days, Dad would give us kids the cars and ride one of our bikes to work, about fifteen miles from home. One time, Dad had to ride one of the younger kid's bikes, which had a banana seat. On the way, he discovered that the brakes didn't work, so every time he came to a stoplight, he would have to ride around in circles until the light changed. When he got to work, he hid the bike in a bush just outside the building. After work, he was pulling it out when a co-worker walked by and commented, "Nice bike." My dad was an incredible example of sacrificial love, always putting his family before himself.

Dad was strict and expected my siblings and me to toe the line. We were only allowed to watch wholesome shows. Our house was a no-swearing zone; not even our friends could get away with swearing. One time, Mom even sent one of my brother's friends home because of it. My mom proudly tells us that she never heard Dad say one swear word in fifty-three years. The closest he came to swearing was once when he was pounding in a nail and with full force, came down directly on his thumb with the hammer. Mom heard him yell, "RRRats!"

My siblings and I were expected to say our prayers, be kind and thoughtful to others, and follow Jesus' teachings. Amidst all this, Mom and Dad found a balance of strictness and fun. We were always encouraged to play outside together. We had lots of fun playing all kinds of games, one of our favorites being wiffleball. There were so many of us that we rarely got bored. On those occasions that we did, with a grin on her face, my mom would say, "If you're bored, I'll give you a dirty, stinkin' rotten job." That worked like a charm. We would backtrack with, "Uh, uh, we're not bored anymore." Then, we'd all scatter.

Our family lived a sacramental life. Mom and Dad had us all baptized as newborns and immersed our family in the faith very intentionally. We went to Mass every Sunday and regularly went to reconciliation. Our family closely followed the liturgical calendar. We always gave up something for Lent and were even expected to be somber on Good Friday. That was okay with us because on Easter Sunday we knew how to celebrate. We'd start the morning by going to Mass together, then gather around our table to share a delicious meal. We would later enjoy an Easter egg hunt and eat lots of candy.

My parents chose to send us to Catholic Schools in both

Nebraska and Washington. I went to Saint Bernadette's from first through fifth grade and then to Saint Michael's for junior high. I loved it there. Everyone was so friendly and welcomed me into the group. It was there that I developed my love for basketball. I felt as if I grew, especially with the discovery of basketball. Being on a team and learning to work together in that way was new to me. I loved it.

Mom was the perfect homemaker. She would get up early to make breakfast, pack lunches, including my dad's, and then get us off to school. We'd return home to snacks and a great dinner made from scratch.

Mom spent a lot of her days volunteering at Saint Michael's. She also held a couple of jobs. Mom taught about pioneer living and would create pioneer experiences in the classrooms. She also had a local television series where she talked about pioneer life. My mom was so into pioneer life that she even went on a ten-day wagon train adventure with her best friend, Sandy. Mom was amazing. She had endless energy. She was able to help her community and experience the joy of life without missing a beat at home.

I was a serious student, so much so that one weekend when I was in junior high, I spent most of the weekend upstairs in my room studying. There was a school carnival on Sunday evening, and the family was going. When my dad told me we'd be leaving soon, I told him, "I'm going to stay home and study." His face got red. "Enough is enough!" He scooped me up over his shoulder, carried me down the stairs, and plopped me in the car saying, "You're going, and you're going to have fun whether you like it or not!" I no longer had a say, because Dad got behind the wheel and we were off.

I didn't have a rebellious spirit. My mom rhetorically used to ask Dad, "Is she a normal teenager? She never gets in trouble." Then, one day, she got a letter in the mail from the high school stating that I was on "Step One." Step One was the first action taken for a school offense, and it was to notify the parents. I came home that day, and Mom questioned me about it. My mom said I had a look of mortification on my face. She couldn't help herself, so she sternly stared me down for a moment, then shouted with elation, "Yes! She IS a normal kid!"

When my siblings and I each graduated from the Catholic grade school, we went on to the local public high school. Sports became a central part of our family, and Mom and Dad proudly went to all our games. Since we no longer went to a Catholic school, Mom and Dad kept us engaged in church life through attending youth group, which included taking classes to prepare each of us for the Sacrament of Confirmation. I graduated from high school and, being that I was still a homebody, I chose to attend Saint Martin's College, which was just ten minutes down the road. My parents were supportive of my decision as it was a Catholic College, and I would live at home. Beyond that, Mom knew Saint Martin's from the inside. She had fond memories of working in the cafeteria by cooking and serving the Monks their dinner. She had built friendships with the very Monks that would be my teachers. The bonus of going to college close to home meant that Mom and Dad could go to my basketball games as I had made the team and would be playing for the Saints. It was a win-win for everyone.

During my junior year at college, I ran into Steve Robbins, who just so happened to be my high school crush. We went to different colleges, but they were both in our hometown. It was a Sunday, and I had decided to go to the evening Mass on campus. That weekend, Steve had played in a soccer tournament and hadn't had the opportunity to go to Mass because of it. So, he went to the evening Mass at Saint Martin's too. After Mass, Steve and I ran into each other. He said, "Hi," and asked me if I went to school here. I said, "Yes," and to my delight, we started talking. Steve knew I had played basketball in high school and asked if I still played. I told him I did, and he said, "I'll come to your next game." He did and continued coming to my games for the rest of my college career.

It was also during my junior year that a friend introduced me to a charismatic healing prayer ministry. I had been looking for a way to deepen my faith, and this opportunity interested me. The group's purpose was to form prayer teams that would go out to churches, retreats, or upon request, individual homes, to pray with people in need of healing. The classes and retreats helped me to connect to God in a new way. As we prayed with people in teams, I could feel the Holy Spirit working through us and witnessed how He ministered to them. At times, we would pray for one another, and I experienced God's presence and His love for me in a way I never had before. It was invigorating.

After graduating from college, I was hired at Saint Joseph Catholic School and began preparing for my first fourth-grade classroom. Saint Joseph's was two hours away from home. It was the first time I lived away from my family. While I enjoyed teaching, I was homesick. I'd talk to Steve every night, and most weekends, he would come down to visit. By the end of that year, I had decided I wanted to return home. When a fourth-grade position became available at Saint Michael's School, my alma mater, I jumped on it. God was good, and I got the job. I was home and happy.

By my third year at Saint Michael's, this very tall, confident woman with a spike hairstyle got hired as the second-grade teacher. At first, I wasn't sure what to think of her, but we hit it off right from the get-go. We ended up team teaching and became friends and prayer partners. That tall, confident woman was Mary. Although we only got to teach one year together, it was the start of what became a life-long friendship. I continued teaching until Steve and I married. Just a little over a year into our marriage, we had our first child, Samuel Joseph. Over the next seventeen years, we welcomed Amy, Rose, Beth, Rebekah, Hannah, Sarah, and Jonathan into the Robbins' nest.

When it came to teaching our children faith and morals, we followed in our parents' footsteps. Steve, too, was brought up in a large Catholic family with parents who also intentionally raised their children in the Catholic faith, and we committed to doing the same. Admittedly, our years together have come with their fair share of challenges, but also with too many blessings to count.

Love God by Serving Others

***

Mary's Memory

"Service with a Smile"

I was born into a military family. My dad grew up on a farm in Osage, Minnesota. Having lost his mother at the age of twelve, he stayed at the farm after high school to help his father and to see his younger sister through high school. He was then eager to move on to new adventures. At twenty-one, one day, he opened the mailbox and found his draft notice. He put it back into the box, went to the recruiting office, and promptly joined the Air Force, hoping to become a pilot like his older brothers. He ended up making a twenty-two-year career out of it.

As for my mom, she grew up in Crawfordsville, which is a small town in Indiana. Her dream was to become a nurse and travel. So, she started her education at Purdue University and finished at Saint Elizabeth's, where she got her Nursing Degree. She then joined the Air Force. Her dream was unexpectedly cut short; however, when she met my dad. She says that while sitting at a bar with a friend, a handsome gentleman tapped her on the shoulder and said, "Are you the Ann Hutson that everyone's talking about?" She replied, "Yes," and agreed to a date.

Dad's version is that he heard about a beautiful nurse on the base named Ann Hutson, so when he saw her at the bar, he made his move. He adds that when he knocked on her door on their first date, and she answered, there was a man in her apartment ironing her uniform behind her. He thought that was hilarious and knew he had met his match - the two dated for the next six weeks.

Then, Mom got orders to the Philippines. She packed up and shipped all her belongings. They arrived, but she did not. Instead, my parents went to the courthouse and got married. They agreed to marry in the church later. Mom was twenty-two, and Dad was twenty-six. This decision ended my mom's service in the Air Force because, at that time, married women were not allowed to serve. Mom always quipped that her sewing machine saw more of the world than she did. Though she would also say that Dad was her best birthday present because they got married just one day before her birthday.

They didn't waste any time starting a family. Within the year, my oldest brother J.C. was born in Texas. Two years after J.C., my sister Margaret was born and then two years later, my brother Jim came along while Dad was stationed in Illinois. Once again, my dad was given orders to move. This time, he was stationed in Denver, Colorado, where I surprised them a month early, arriving on Christmas Eve.

When I was still a baby Dad was sent to war. My parents packed us up and moved the family to Crawfordsville, so my mom could be supported by her family while Dad was at war. In 1967, Dad returned from Vietnam and was stationed at McChord Air Force Base in Tacoma, Washington. There, Dad flew C-141s, a cargo plane. He would be home for two weeks, then gone two weeks, home for two weeks, then gone for two.

I loved picking Dad up from the airport. He always had his flight suit on, with zippered pockets all over it. He would hide little goodies in one of his pockets for each of us. I remember hugging him and then searching his pockets zipper by zipper until I found what he brought me. It was so much fun.

My parents loved the Pacific Northwest, especially Dad. He loved the beauty of Mount Rainier, Puget Sound, and the Pacific Ocean. He wanted everyone he loved to see the area, so he would invite all his family and friends out, and they took him up on it too. Then, when Dad gave people the tour of the area, he would say, "Most folks show people the sights, but I'm going to show you the Sound." Then, he'd throw his head back and laugh. My family never moved again. We were home.

My siblings and I went to the local public schools. We attended Mass as a family at the local high school until the archdiocese built Saint John Bosco Catholic Church. It was there that I received the Sacraments of Reconciliation, Communion, and Confirmation. I was also eventually married in that parish.

My mom and dad lived their faith helping others. Lending a hand was a priority in our home. My dad told people that if they needed anything, "our door was open, and our refrigerator was friendly." Through the years, I remember having many guests sitting around our table. Their hospitality was one of the ways that my parents showed my siblings and me that we love God by serving others.

Dad was the organizer when many of the houses in our aging neighborhood needed new roofs. He negotiated bulk pricing for all the shingles and materials required for five homes and then organized a neighborhood work crew each weekend to replace the roofs one by one. Many of the men were out of town on military missions, but everyone helped when they could. Having been a hard-working farm boy, Dad had the skills needed and taught these skills to our neighbors, one house at a time, until everyone had a new roof.

Mom was an Emergency Room nurse and freely shared her knowledge and skills. Many a parent brought their children to our home seeking first aid. Many a phone call was taken, at all hours of the day and night, with worried moms seeking advice. We loved and served our neighbors.

Growing up, I was a sensitive child with a tender heart who struggled through the public school system because of it. When switching from elementary school to junior high, rather than sending me on to the junior high school my siblings went to, my parents sent me to a Catholic school and then on to the local Catholic high school. My life changed as I learned more about the God I was taught to serve.

During these years, I met my four lifelong friends. We became so tight that our parents affectionately called us "the girls." I also met my two mentors, Mr. and Mrs. Sonneman, who both became my confirmation sponsors and were instrumental in helping me to become the person I am today. Mr. Sonneman was my eighth-grade Social Studies teacher, and his wife was my first-grade teacher. Honestly, I cannot say enough about what they did to bring God alive for me.

For example, each summer, they would take my friends and me out to their house, a small cabin off Lake Saint Claire. There, Mr. Sonneman played the guitar and led us in singing our favorite church songs around the campfire, and he and Mrs. Sonneman would field all kinds of questions about faith or get us thinking about what it means to be Catholic. These gatherings went on into our college years.

During high school, I took advantage of the opportunities it provided for me to do what I learned at home. I became the president of Campus Ministry and led the student body in charitable events like food drives that would stock up the local food bank and volunteered in a local nursing home where I helped develop activities for residents in which to participate. I also became a Eucharistic Minister to serve at the school Masses. At the end of my senior year, I received the Community Service Award. I only mention this because you will soon see how that comes full circle.

When it came time to go to college, four of us "girls" attended Washington State University together. I lived with two of them in the dorm and an apartment, as we each earned our teaching degrees. One of my favorite things we did together was work on Search Retreats at the Catholic Church on campus. They were put on twice a year, one in the fall and one in the spring, and we enjoyed serving at both of them. My friends and I loved being crew members. Crew members were the people who worked behind the scenes to provide food for everyone and then cleaned up behind them. We would also put on skits to help reinforce what the retreatants were learning. But what was really fun was that we were like "Secret Santas" because we would each adopt a team leader and their group. Then, throughout the retreat, we would sneak into their cabin or next meeting place and surprise them with a special little somethin' somethin'. By the end of the retreat, we were exhausted but so happy that we did it.

My junior year came with great sorrow as well as joy. While I lost Mr. Sonneman to cancer, I met my future husband, Aaron. My dorm was becoming coed for the first time. The Resident Assistants (R.A.s) had sponsors to help with the changeover. So, I volunteered to work as a sponsor for the R.A. of my floor, who turned out to be Aaron. Aaron helped me through the loss of Mr. Sonneman. It brought us closer together.

At our first meeting, it was love at first sight! I knew that I had found my husband. Fun fact - one of my lifelong friends was also an R.A. in the same dorm. All of the R.A.s arrived at the dorm before the sponsors, so my friend met Aaron before I did. During that time, all the R.A.s played a game of who would date who in the government. My friend predicted that we would not only date but Aaron and I would marry. To this day, she does not know why she thought that, but like me, she just knew - and we were both right!

During our time in the dorm, Aaron asked me if I would be interested in working at the County Crisis Line. He told me that I could try it without committing because many people find out that it's not for them after trying it and invited me to take a one-day class to prepare me. The thought of working the Crisis Line scared me because it was the real deal. However, knowing that I would serve others clinched it, so I agreed, took the class with him, and then started working the Crisis Line.

I was terrified every time the phone rang. I was afraid that at the other end was a suicide call, but I pushed myself past my fears, and I'm glad I did. It was a gratifying experience because I was there for people when they felt as if they had no one else to talk to them through their crisis. After spending so much time together, to my delight, Aaron and I became college sweethearts before the year's end.

My senior year was challenging because Aaron was no longer on campus as he was doing his student teaching at home. Rather than sitting around depressed, I decided to follow my advisor's recommendation to enhance my resume. So, I talked to a friend from one of my Child and Family Studies classes. We had recently learned about "latchkey" children. A latchkey child was a child who went home after school to an empty house. It was in that class that I learned that I was one.

In our conversation, I asked my friend if she would help me design and potentially implement a Latchkey Program. The program would take place once a week at the local elementary school between three and six o'clock, which was about the time between the end of school and when parents got off work. She agreed, and we got to work putting together a safe and fun alternative for children who would otherwise go home to an empty house.

We approached the local elementary school principal with our six-week program. When he asked why we wanted to do it, my answer was, "Because growing up, I was a latchkey child, and if it weren't for Mrs. Allen, my elderly next-door neighbor, I would have gone home to an empty house. It was a joy to go to her house, and I want to give the children of your school that same gift." He agreed to let us pilot our program. It went so well that when we finished, the parents wanted the program to continue. So, what started as just a project meant to enhance a couple of resumes ended up meeting one community's needs.

Aaron finished his student teaching by Christmas of 1985 and graduated. By the time I came home that Christmas, I had completed all of my classes on campus and was ready to start my student teaching. I first taught in a second-grade classroom, followed by the second round of student teaching in a gifted fourth-grade classroom. I finally finished my student teaching in May of 1986 and was excited to graduate. To my surprise, Dad borrowed his friend's jet and flew Mom, Margaret, Aaron, and me to Washington State University, so we didn't have to drive the six-hour trip back to campus for graduation. Dad let his future son-in-law ride in the cockpit with him. To this day, Aaron lights up at the memory.

The following spring, on March 14, 1987, I became Aaron's wife. We were still in the process of finding jobs, so we had an acute lack of money, but looking back on it, we knew something was on the horizon, and we were in love. Love conquers all, right? We still laugh about the time we went to the grocery store and stood debating whether or not we could afford to buy a spatula that cost a dollar - we couldn't and didn't!

Before we had children, Aaron and I had seven lovely years together. During that time, we bought our first house. It was old, so we refurbished it, being careful to maintain its charm. We created a lovely backyard with a deck for enjoying time with family and friends.

As Aaron was a teacher, too, we both chose to work in Catholic Schools. At the time, many Catholic schools were in danger of closing due to low attendance and funding. Since Catholic schools changed my world, we wanted to do our part to keep them alive.

Unfortunately, the first school that I worked at did end up closing at the end of that year, despite our best efforts to keep it going. However, the first school Aaron worked at gained me a friend. He worked at Saint Michael's, which coincidentally was precisely where Laurie worked, and Aaron just knew we would become fast friends - which we did!

The following school year, Saint Patrick's hired me as a fourth-grade teacher. When Aaron got the opportunity to teach there also, he took it, as the commute to Saint Michael's was long. Saint Patrick's was the first place we had the joy of working together. However, when a second-grade position opened up at Saint Michael's, I took it, as that was the grade I wanted to teach. This is where Laurie and I met and team-taught together for one glorious year. Aaron left Saint Patrick's as well. He took a high school position at my alma mater.

A job in the Community Service Department opened up at that same school just one year later. I applied and got hired by the very teacher who had given me that Community Service Award nine years before. It was an honor to work with a woman who had so influenced my life. Again, Aaron and I found ourselves teaching at the same school. I spent two years teaching there before getting pregnant with our firstborn, Patrick. Aaron and I decided that it would be best for our family if I left teaching and became a full-time mom - and it was! Over the course of the next ten years, we welcomed six more children. Baby Faith, Kathleen, Baby Hope,

Maggie, Baby John Kirby, and Baby Love. We cherish Patrick, Kathleen, and Maggie here on earth, as we await with anticipation, the reunion with our four little saints in heaven.

When it came to teaching our children faith and morals, we followed in our parents' footsteps. Aaron was also raised in a Catholic family with parents who taught the importance of loving God by serving others. We committed to doing the same. Admittedly, our years together have had some heart-wrenching challenges - but they have also brimmed with countless blessings!

Our Bios

***

Laurie Robbins attended Saint Martin's University where she earned her Bachelor of Arts in Elementary Education with a minor in English and Language Arts. She went on to earn her Master of Education through Lesley University. Laurie taught fourth grade in the Seattle Archdiocese for three years. Laurie now resides in Centralia, Washington with her husband Steve of thirty-two years. They have been blessed with eight incredible children, two terrific sons-in-law, and two beautiful grandchildren. Life is very good.

Mary Rogers attended Washington State University, where she became a proud "Coug." While there, she earned her Bachelor of Arts in Elementary Education with a minor in Child and Family Studies. Mary taught the second, third, and fourth grades in the Seattle Archdiocese as well as Community Service at a Catholic High School. Mary now resides in Tacoma, Washington with her husband Aaron of thirty-seven years. They cherish their three passionate and kind-hearted children, have rescued and loved their fifteen dog babies, and look forward to hugging their four little ones in heaven.

Endnotes

***

1. Saint-Exupéry, A. de, & Woods, K. (1971). Chapter 21. In *The Little Prince* (pp. 70–70). essay, Harcourt Brace & World, Inc.

2. www.littleflower.ie/our-patron-st-therese-of lisieux?gclid=CjwKCAjwq4imBhBQEiwA9Nx1BnRue4uFW0VZgW Al0pe999gHkM6INGcfbE9Fpce7gOhQSMfvnJgrJhoCvD8QAvD_Bw E. Accessed 27 July 2023.

3. https://www.google.com/search?tbm=vid&sxsrf=AB5stBhmbvTYwcw Ofv3_okIkh5zVfGEekg%3A1691187565419&q=the%2Bhymn%2Bi% 2Bhave%2Bloved%2Byou%2Bwith%2Ban%2Beverlasting%2Blove&s a=X&ved=2ahUKEwiii9fQhMSAAxXoMEQIHS27B6wQ8ccDegQIE RAJ&biw=1268&bih=527&dpr=1#fpstate=ive&vld=cid:b10c5fe8,vid: Fmn_QgeIpTs

4. Kelly, Matthew. Rediscovering the Saints: 25 Questions That Will Change Your Life. Blue Sparrow, 2019.

5. Kelly, Matthew. Rediscovering the Saints: 25 Questions That Will Change Your Life. Blue Sparrow, 2019.

6. Cullinan, Bernice. "Reading with Your Child." *Reading Rockets*, www.readingrockets.org/article/reading-your-child. Accessed 26 July 2023.

7. Kelly, Matthew. Rediscovering the Saints: 25 Questions That Will Change Your Life. Blue Sparrow, 2019.

8. "1915 Penny - Scottish Country Dance of the Day." *Scdancethemes*, Curious Magpie Designs, www.scottishcountrydanceoftheday.com/daysoftheyear/1915penny#:~: text=The%20original%20phrase%20was%20%22see,the%20person%2 0who%20found%20it. Accessed 12 Oct. 2023

9. DuFrene, Troy. "Two Boats and a Helicopter." *Two Boats and a Helicopter*, 13 Jan. 2021, sfcompassion.com/two-boats-and-a-helicopter/.

10. Facing the Giants. Written by Alex Kendrick and Stephen Kendrick, Directed by Alex Kendrick, Music by Mark Willard, Performances by Alex Kendrick, Shannen Fields, Tracy Goode, James Blackwell, Bailey Cave, Jim McBride, and Jason McCloud, Production company Sherwood Pictures Provident Films and Caramel Entertainment Kendrick Brothers Group, Distributed by Samuel Goldwyn Films and Destination Films, Filmed in the U.S.A., September 29, 2006.

11. "O Holy Night." *Wikipedia*, Wikimedia Foundation, 9 Sept. 2023, en.wikipedia.org/wiki/O_Holy_Night.

12. "Prayer of St. Francis, (Make Me a Channel of Your Peace) Sung by Angelina, EWTN." *Prayer of St. Francis, (Make Me A Channel of Your Peace) Sung by Angelina, EWTN*, 8 Apr. 2008, www.youtube.com/watch?v=ZI1Gst7pEqc.

13. "Catholic News, TV, Radio: EWTN." *EWTN Global Catholic Television Network*, EWTN Global Catholic Television Network, www.ewtn.com/. Accessed 22 Sept. 2023.

14. Admin. (n.d.). *Lyrics, videos and stories behind hymns. – Lyrics, Videos and Stories Behind Hymns.* https://christianmusicandhymns.com/2022/11/o-be-careful-little-eyes-lyrics-story-and-video.html

15. "Two-Face." *DC*, DC, www.dc.com/characters/two-face. Accessed 1 Nov. 2023.

16. Chicks, Social. "How to Be Authentic in the Noise of Traffic." *How to Be Authentic in the Noise of Traffic*, 15 Aug. 2016, www.mainstreetcommunications.ca/2015/01/19/how-to-be-authentic-in-the-noise-of-traffic/.

Made in the USA
Monee, IL
01 August 2024